FRUIT CAKE

FRUIT CAKE

RECIPES FOR THE CURIOUS BAKER

JASON SCHREIBER

WILLIAM MORROW

An Imprint of HarperCollinsPublishers

FOR BIM AND SAM

First to show was sweet Clement

Richard often came and went

Unlike Sal who settled in

Instantly becoming kin

Thinking there was room for more

Florence flitted through the door

Leon, Gerald, Evan, Ray—

It seems their numbers grow each day

Exhausted as I try and try

Still these fruit flies will not die

CONTENTS

ix   FOREWORD BY MARTHA STEWART

1   ALLOW ME TO INTRODUCE MYSELF

3   GETTING STARTED

15   CONSTANT CRAVINGS

65   OUT OF HAND

99   SHOWSTOPPERS

149   ALL RISE

189   SOAKED

223   THE BASICS

251   FILE UNDER: IT TAKES A VILLAGE

253   CONVERSION CHART

255   INDEX

FOREWORD

The last time I worked with Jason Schreiber, a longtime, beloved contributor to the food departments of our magazine, our books, and our television shows, was for a Christmas project for *Martha Stewart Living* in December 2019. Jason and I spent a busy week creating a magnificent Gingerbread "Village." Jason's skill as a baker, architect, designer, and decorator was in full throttle and the project was a beautiful success. During that time, as we were ensconced up to our elbows in gingerbread, Jason spoke excitedly about a personal project, his first book, *Fruit Cake*.

When I received the galley of this book, I immediately understood Jason's excitement. This is a very serious accomplishment, and a wonderful first book for a talented and erudite baker. Jason's love of shaking up tradition is evident, and adding fruits to bolster flavors in familiar baked goods is creative and groundbreaking. I became enamored of the idea of a new version, a modern take, on my childhood fruitcake memory cemented in my favorite fruitcake, Mrs. Maus's Fruitcake.

Reading through the seventy-five intriguing recipes, I couldn't wait to try each and every one of them. I recently planted a fruit tree orchard—plums, peaches, apricots, cherries, apples, pears, persimmons, quince, and even Asian pears—and enlarged my number of berry bushes and plants (raspberries, black raspberries, blackberries, gooseberries, currants, blueberries, and strawberries). One of my goals is to use my berries in Jason's Blackberry Breton and my plethora of gooseberries in his crumb cakes. Even my yuzu lemons have a new recipe in which to star!

Jason's recipes are well written, his directions are clear, and the ingredients are attainable. That said, many of Jason's comments are a bit iconoclastic, and he often questions common wisdom, steering us instead to experiment, try new combinations of flavors, and expand our baking vocabulary.

Thank you, Jason, for this collection of mouthwatering recipes for cakes we have not yet tasted, but certainly will.

—Martha Stewart

ALLOW ME TO INTRODUCE MYSELF

I have, at last check, two pints of red currants, six oranges, eight kiwis, three bananas, and at least a dozen limes in my refrigerator. There's butter, too—some of it is cultured—and not one but two half-empty cartons of eggs. There are easily six types of sugar in my pantry, not to mention the flours (there had been five, but I've finally finished the spelt) and three open bottles of the exact same vanilla. My freezer is full of compost and coconuts.

It's entirely possible I'm a hoarder.

I used to shop like a normal person, but then I became a food stylist. I shop from photoshoot garbage now. It's a weird way to live: not quite dumpster-diving for high-end ingredients. The spoils are as extravagant as they are sundry, which leads to a bizarrely stocked kitchen like mine. I can't stand to see such things wasted, so I take them home, imagining new lives for them—anything to stave off the dreaded compost bin. It's an office perk and a curse rolled into one.

At first I tried to just eat everything as quickly as I could, but there are only so many mangoes a man can force-feed himself. It became clear there was only one solution, and it was the one that was with me all along.

I was born in a gingerbread house, just another bun in the proverbial oven. It's not believable but it gets the point across; I can't remember a time when baking wasn't important to me. It started inauspiciously enough with some take or another on one-bowl brownies, but things quickly got out of hand. Lots of nine-year-olds have lemonade stands. I made crepes to order. Yes, there are photos. No, I won't show you.

(Note to self: What about a guava crepe cake?)

Years later, even when I was quite literally surrounded by cakes for most of my waking hours during the five years I worked with pastry chef Ron Ben-Israel, I never seemed to grow tired of them. The staff would pile into buckets scraps that had been trimmed from some of the most extravagant cakes in all of New York, and like so many hogs to the feeding trough, we would fight for the most succulent morsels. The carrot cake couldn't last a day. It's no secret it was the pineapple that made it so good. We couldn't have cared less about the carrots.

As I've wended my way since then, I haven't changed my tune. I've had the good fortune of landing jobs at veritable institutions like Martha Stewart Living Omnimedia. There's nothing quite like watching from just off camera as Martha makes one of your recipes. Knees bent nervously, lower, and lower still. I paid in anxiety for the privilege of learning, not only from Martha but from her team of exceptional cooks, how to make it work and how to recover from the inevitable blunder. Lying on the cold concrete floor is one way. It's surprisingly restorative.

And since Martha doesn't waste a thing, my time there certainly did nothing for my stockpiling compulsions. Where there are berries there could be jam, once you know how to make it. Or a shortcake. Wouldn't that be nice?

I'm here to offer modern recipes planted firmly in the idea that nature's wares can be the star of every cake. And I'm willing to use up every goddamn thing in my refrigerator to prove it.

GETTING STARTED

YOUR KITCHEN IS NOT ROOM TEMPERATURE, AND OTHER FOLLIES

Home kitchens are not laboratories, though it's fun to pretend they are. We make assumptions and work on blind faith that standards exist to serve us. Nothing is as it seems.

YOUR KITCHEN IS NOT ROOM TEMPERATURE

It's November, and for the first time in weeks I haven't even turned on the oven. I also haven't turned on the heat, and the bottom line is: I'm freezing. I would go get a sweater, but every time I get up from my computer, I lose my train of thought. Besides, I'm trying to illustrate a point. My kitchen is cold as the dickens today; two months ago it was sweltry hot.

Almost every baking recipe begins with the same request that you bring the ingredients to room temperature, but the temperature of the room is never given. A too-cold room probably won't end in disaster, but it might keep your eggs and butter from creaming together beautifully or cause your yeasted dough to rise more slowly than expected. A too-hot room could wreak havoc on a temperamental frosting or even cause butter to melt instead of soften. The world goes on.

While I won't argue that you should change the temperature of your room, I will suggest you change the temperature of your ingredients by warming or cooling them as needed. Eggs can easily be warmed in a bowl of hot water for 10 minutes or so to take the chill off. Butter and the like can be microwaved in 10-second increments or set in a warm spot near the stove until they're just malleable but not melting. Warm milk in the microwave, or on the stove over gentle heat, to a temperature that can only be described as "tepid." Finally, when the summer heat takes hold, find a cool spot for your butter to relax and refrigerate if it softens too quickly.

YOUR OVEN IS INACCURATE

And so is mine. They're not designed to be precision instruments. Using an oven thermometer may help you identify its quirks and hot spots, but it won't solve the underlying issue, which is that in the time it takes to bake a cake, the temperature inside your oven will vary drastically—by as much as 25°F (about 14°C) in either direction—from whatever you set it to. There's not much to be done other than remember that people have been baking for thousands of years without a fuss. Keep an eye, or a nose, on what's going on inside the oven as you bake. Adjust the time, tent with foil, and rotate your pans as needed. You can always adjust the temperature, too, but it's same-same but different, as it were. My best advice: Preheat, the longer the better. Temperature fluctuation tends to decrease the longer an oven runs.

YOUR MEASUREMENTS ARE OFF

While most of the rest of the world has moved on to the metric system, we in the United States are holdouts on measuring by the cup. I'll admit it has its advantages. I can quickly grab a scoop of this or two of that without stopping to think or even fully open a container. All that scooping can lead to a fair amount of inconsistency if your system isn't methodical, but user error is far from the only cause of unreliable measurements.

I recently conducted a little study, because although I'm on a deadline, I'm also easily distracted. I measured the same ingredient (sugar) using all of my measuring cups and spoons. I have many (see: hoarder, above). I'll cut to the chase: No two measuring cups were alike. Even when I switched to metric, my three scales couldn't completely agree, though admittedly they were much closer. I've been baking with these tools *for years* and never bothered to check if they were doing their jobs well. I can't say I've ever had a major problem, either. Could it be that nothing matters?

Here's the thing: Our kitchens are different. We all measure with different tools, use different ingredients, and put things in different ovens. And yet somehow we're able to arrive at similar results. This is why baking is an art and not strictly a science. Use the tools that make you the most comfortable, and bake with all your senses. When you measure, be careful and at least you'll be consistent. Here's how I go about it . . .

MEASURE BY MEASURE

There are three basic categories that need to be measured while baking: things that are liquid, things that are not, and things that you use in small quantities.

LIQUIDS

Liquids flow more or less like water. Honey and molasses are liquids, though just barely. Yogurt, it depends. As a general rule, liquids move to fill the measuring container of their own accord, forming a nominally flat surface (hold this thought). We measure them using liquid measuring cups, which look like pitchers.* Place the cup on a flat surface and read the measurement from the side at eye level, being mindful of the meniscus, the subtle curve formed at the top of the liquid. Measure from its center, which may be lower or higher than it appears on the edges, depending on the viscosity of the liquid. Liquid measurements are recorded in cups and fluid ounces in the United States, or milliliters pretty much everywhere else.

"DRY" GOODS

In the United States, we measure things that aren't liquids with dry measuring cups, but the techniques are slightly different depending on what it is you're measuring. Most of the rest of the world would prefer to weigh these ingredients (more on that later).

- **Powders,** such as flour, cornstarch, or confectioners' sugar, should be scooped and leveled to the top of the cup using a flat blade or metal spatula. It's good practice to briefly stir whatever it is you're measuring in its container before scooping so that it's not overly compacted. You may have been taught to sift flours before measuring. I usually can't be bothered to do so, and I find stirring in the container to be just as effective—unless a recipe specifies otherwise.

* *Or ewers, if you're doing a crossword puzzle.*

the outside of the scoop, which is not what you intended to measure.

- **Awkward items,** like berries, nuts, chocolate, and herbs, are nearly impossible to measure effectively by volume. Loosely place them into the measuring scoop, filling it more or less to the brim, or a little over. You'll never get them to fit perfectly, and it will never matter.

SMALL QUANTITIES

There are a handful of ingredients we use in such small quantities that measuring according to the categories above simply doesn't make sense, such as leaveners, salt, and extracts. These items can be liquid or dry, and we measure them with spoons, which in the United States are in increments by tablespoon, teaspoon, and so on. The rest of the world uses milliliters. Fill the spoon to the top and level using a blade or the edge of the box if the ingredient is a powder. You can also weigh these items, of course.

- **Granules,** such as granulated sugar, cornmeal, or rice, can generally be scooped and leveled simply by shaking off the excess, but using a blade certainly won't hurt. It's not strictly necessary to stir in the container before you measure, either.
- **Brown sugars,** both light and dark, should be packed into the measuring scoop and flattened with the palm of your hand. Use enough pressure so that the puck of sugar holds its shape when you tap it out of the scoop.
- **Viscous ingredients,** like yogurt, pumpkin puree, and sour cream, should be spooned into the measuring scoop and leveled with a blade or spatula. Be careful to clean off

WEIGHTS

If you're an enthusiastic baker, a professional, or part of the global majority, you may prefer to measure by weight. Yes, it's a far more precise method, but I'll confess that even after years of working in professional kitchens, I continue to think in terms of U.S. cups and spoons when I'm developing recipes. I'm including gram measurements for the rest of you. About weights I will say only this: Even digital scales are only so accurate, and there is little consensus about exact volume-to-gram conversions. The conversions I use in this book are the ones I've measured in my own kitchen and are as accurate to my methods as can be.

INGREDIENTS

What comes out of your oven depends in large part on what you put into it. Choosing the right ingredients can be a challenge. Here's what to look for:

FLOURS

For such a staple item there sure are a lot to choose from.

- **All-purpose flour** is just that, a middle-of-the-road solution that works in most instances. I prefer unbleached, unbromated* all-purpose flour that has been minimally processed. Different brands of all-purpose flour have different amounts of protein. I prefer ones on the high end of the spectrum, such as Heckers, Ceresota, or King Arthur, which have protein counts of about 11.5 percent.
- **Bread flour** has the highest protein count of all, which is what gives bread its chew. I use it sparingly in this book to add structure to certain cakes and yeasted doughs. I prefer unbleached, unbromated bread flour, such as King Arthur Bread Flour, which has a protein count of 12.7 percent.
- **Cake flour** has a low protein count (generally about 7 to 8 percent), which results in less gluten development. In the United States it is typically bleached, a chemical process that affects the way the starch molecules absorb moisture and bond with fats. This results in cakes that have a softer texture, a more even crumb, and a higher rise than those made with unbleached flour. I use bleached, unbromated cake flour in a handful of recipes in this book where I find it has a meaningful impact. My go-to brand is Swans Down.

  I know that bleached cake flour is not available in all regions. Some bakers may choose to substitute all-purpose flour that has been lightened with cornstarch. I find the best formula for this method to be based on the weight of the flour: For each 113 grams (1 cup) of cake flour called for in a recipe, weigh out an equal amount of all-purpose flour (about a heaping ¾ cup) and add 16 grams (2 tablespoons) of cornstarch.

  Crucially, cake flour is not the same as self-rising flour, which also contains baking powder and salt.
- **Masa harina (prepared corn flour):** Unlike stone-ground cornmeal, this flour comes from corn that has been nixtamalized, an ancient Mesoamerican method of soaking corn in a solution of cal (also known as pickling lime or calcium hydroxide). This makes the nutrients easier to digest, and imbues the corn with the flavor typical of tortillas.
- **Quick-cooking (but not instant) polenta:** Sometimes this Italian-style cornmeal actually says this on the package. If not, get something that's ready in about 2 minutes and isn't labeled "coarse grind."
- **Semolina flour:** You could be forgiven for assuming this coarsely ground flour comes from corn due to its color and texture, but

---

* *Potassium bromate is a dough conditioner that is sometimes added to flour to increase gluten strength and oven spring while reducing mixing times. Because of the potential for adverse health effects, many countries (and the state of California) have banned or regulated its use. As a result, most brands of flour available to consumers are now bromate-free, though it still can be found in some flours sold to commercial bakeries.*

| **1.** MASA HARINA | **2.** STONE-GROUND CORNMEAL | **3.** QUICK-COOKING POLENTA | **4.** CAKE FLOUR |

| **5.** BREAD FLOUR | **6.** SEMOLINA FLOUR | **7.** SPELT FLOUR | **8.** ALL-PURPOSE FLOUR

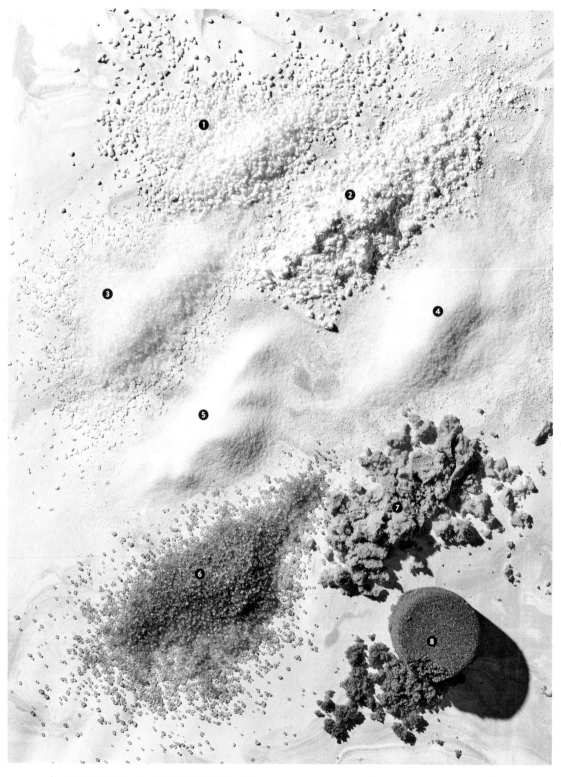

| **1.** PEARL SUGAR | **2.** CONFECTIONERS' SUGAR | **3.** SANDING SUGAR | **4.** GRANULATED SUGAR |
| **5.** SUPERFINE SUGAR | **6.** TURBINADO SUGAR | **7.** LIGHT BROWN SUGAR | **8.** DARK BROWN SUGAR |

it's actually from durum wheat, and is the variety most often used to make Italian pastas and couscous.

- **Spelt flour:** Spelt is an ancient grain that contains less gluten than wheat (but is not gluten free). Each brand of spelt flour is ground slightly differently. I prefer it to be very fine, with a texture similar to cake flour.
- **Stone-ground cornmeal:** This is different from polenta. It's finely ground and behaves more like flour.

SWEETENERS

Sugar does more than make things taste sweet. It is a binder, meaning it helps hold baked goods together, and affects the texture of the final product by making it chewy or crisp. It's also hygroscopic, meaning that it bonds with water, which helps keep baked goods moist and prevent spoilage. Since baking is chemistry at its core, there are minimum amounts of sugar necessary for sweet recipes to work. I tend to steer as close to those minimums as can be, allowing other, more nuanced, flavors to shine.

There many types of sweeteners. These are the varieties I like to have on hand:

- **Brown sugar,** both light and dark, is white sugar that has had molasses added back in and so lends a toffee-like flavor to recipes. It's also slightly more acidic and retains more water than white sugar, which can help make baked goods chewier. Once opened, brown sugar has a tendency to solidify and can become difficult to work with. I like to keep mine in the freezer, which seems to extend its life.
- **Confectioners' sugar** is white sugar that has been finely pulverized into a powder and contains cornstarch to prevent it from clumping. Professionals lovingly refer to it as "10X," because it's been ground ten times. It's also called icing sugar in some parts of the world.
- **Finishing sugars** are designed to look more or less the same going into and coming out of the oven. Since they're mostly used for decoration, they can easily be substituted. I tend toward coarse sanding sugar, turbinado sugar, and pearl sugar, but there are many other types to choose from.
- **Granulated sugar** is the most common sweetener you'll come across in these recipes (and really, any baking recipe). It's made by refining the juice of the sugarcane plant, a complex and multistep process that strips away the molasses and forms naturally occurring sucrose into the crystals we're familiar with. Organic sugar, which is slightly less processed, contains a bit more molasses and tends to be a touch darker in color, but can otherwise be used interchangeably with conventional sugar.
- **Superfine sugar** is granulated sugar with smaller crystals, which helps it dissolve more quickly. In a pinch, you can make a substitute by pulsing granulated sugar in the food processor. The result will be less uniform, but you'll make do. In the UK, superfine sugar is called caster sugar.
- **Syrups,** such as Lyle's Golden Syrup, black treacle, honey, maple syrup, and (gasp!) corn syrup,* are liquid sweeteners that, due to their chemical structure, can last long periods of time without crystalizing. Syrups add a certain gooeyness, prevent crystallization, and increase the shelf life of finished baked goods.

* *I use corn syrup sparingly and for specific reasons. See page 136 for my detailed excuse.*

DAIRY

Dairy is a complicated ingredient that contributes in many different ways to a recipe by adding fat, acidity, protein, and moisture.

- **Butter** needs to taste good. If you wouldn't put it on toast, don't put it in a cake. I like a European style with 83 percent butterfat when I can get it. I use only unsalted butter when I'm baking, though I prefer salted butter for serving.
- **Buttermilk** has undergone a transformation over the years and has little to do with butter these days. It's a cultured product, similar to yogurt, and is almost always marketed as low-fat.
- **Heavy cream** whips the best when it's been formulated to do so and is often sold as "heavy whipping cream," which contains additives such as carrageenan. I prefer cream that is just that: cream, with no other ingredients, such as Natural by Nature. It's harder to find, and a little harder to whip, but I'll take purity over perfection.
- **Milk** should be fresh and not at all sour. I use whole milk in my recipes.
- **Sour cream, crème fraîche, yogurt, cream cheese,** and **mascarpone** are all thicker dairy products that add fat and flavor with less liquid. They should be full fat and high quality, with few, if any, additives.

FATS

You won't get far in a baking book with an aversion to fat.* Aside from the time-honored culinary school mantra "fat is flavor," it's also crucial to the texture and appearance of baked goods. Most of the fat in these recipes comes

from butter and eggs, but I like to switch in other types, such as coconut, safflower, or olive oil, to create interesting flavors or help out with a dairy intolerance. Liquid fats behave very differently from solid fats and serve different purposes in a recipe, the former helping to create a more tender finished product, while the latter can aerate a batter or create a flaky texture.

SALT

Using the right amount of salt is more of an art than a science; we all have different tolerances and tastes. Most of the time I use salt in baked goods as a flavor enhancer, rather than as a flavor of its own. Most of the time, but not always.

One of the biggest challenges when it comes to using salt is that the crystal size of every brand is different, which can lead to very different amounts when you measure by volume. The best brand of salt is the one you feel most comfortable using. For me that's Diamond Crystal kosher salt, which weighs about 3 grams per teaspoon, if you want to be exact. It's what I'm referring to when I call for "coarse salt," which is nearly always.

YEAST

Most of the yeasted recipes in this book use instant yeast. It's my go-to because it's easy to measure, quick to dissolve, and available in most grocery stores. In truth, you can happily use whatever type of yeast you prefer, provided you know how to adjust the quantities and—crucially—the rising times. You can use the chart opposite as a guide.

I generally call for warm milk to dissolve yeast in sweet doughs. Use warmer liquids, around 110°F (43°C), for dry yeast, and cooler liquids, around 95°F (35°C), for fresh yeast.

* Crossword puzzle: oleo. Don't expect my help after Tuesday.

IF A RECIPE CALLS FOR	USE	OR
1 ounce (2 tablespoons, 28 grams) fresh yeast	1 tablespoon (1⅓ envelopes, 9.3 grams) active dry yeast	2 teaspoons (scant 1 envelope, 6.2 grams) instant yeast
	The dough will rise more slowly, so use visual cues rather than noted timing to determine when to proceed with the next step in the recipe.	
2¼ teaspoons (1 envelope, 7 grams) active dry yeast	1½ teaspoons (4.7 grams) instant yeast	¾ ounce (1½ tablespoons, 21 grams) fresh yeast
	The dough will rise faster, so use visual cues rather than noted timing to determine when to proceed with the next step in the recipe.	
1 teaspoon (3 grams) active dry yeast	¾ teaspoon (2.3 grams) instant yeast	⅓ ounce (2 teaspoons, 9.3 grams) fresh yeast
	The dough will rise faster, so use visual cues rather than noted timing to determine when to proceed with the next step in the recipe.	
2¼ teaspoons (1 envelope, 7 grams) instant yeast	3½ teaspoons (11 grams) active dry yeast	2 tablespoons plus 1 teaspoon (heaping 1 ounce, 33 grams) fresh yeast
	The dough will rise more slowly, so use visual cues rather than noted timing to determine when to proceed with the next step in the recipe.	
1 teaspoon (3 grams) instant yeast	1½ teaspoons (4.5 grams) active dry yeast	1 tablespoon (½ ounce, 14 grams) fresh yeast
	The dough will rise more slowly, so use visual cues rather than noted timing to determine when to proceed with the next step in the recipe.	

SOME FINAL CLARIFICATIONS

- Cardamom: To freshly grind, crack the green pods and discard, then grind the seeds. I use a mortar and pestle.
- Chocolate: Always use the best quality you can get. I prefer couverture chocolate, which has a higher percentage of cocoa butter and melts more easily. It's usually sold in small wafers or *pistoles*. (The alternative is baking chocolate, which is designed to hold its shape in the oven. Good for cookies, but not as good for cakes.) Since couverture isn't always easy to find, I'd suggest unflavored chocolate candy bars as an alternative. These days they're usually labeled by their cacao content, just like fancy couverture chocolate is, and many are fair trade. I like to use something in the 65% to 70% cacao range, unless otherwise noted, which I think is just sweet enough for most applications.

- **Dried cherries:** There are quite a lot of dried cherries in these recipes, both sweet and tart. Dried tart cherries are sometimes sold as "dried sour cherries" and you can use them interchangeably. Dried sweet cherries might be labeled "dried Bing cherries." I generally try to avoid using *sweetened* dried cherries, which have added sugar, but that's a personal preference.
- **Eggs:** I use large eggs in my recipes, which weigh about 60 grams in their shells, 50 without. Use the freshest, least-processed eggs you can find—pasture raised, if you can get them. The hens thank you.
- **Nutmeg:** When grating and measuring nutmeg is too big a burden to bear, but using preground is simply unthinkable, I grate mine on a rasp grater directly into the bowl at a steady clip of about two back-and-forths per second. Five seconds yields about ¼ teaspoon (0.5 gram).
- **Pure vanilla extract,** not imitation.
- **Zesting:** Wash the fruit well and use a rasp grater to remove only the outermost layer of peel. If you've exposed any white pith, you've gone way too far. After zesting, the fruit should be a velvety version of the color it once was.

KITCHEN TOOLS

I could write a whole book about what tools you should (and shouldn't) have in your kitchen. No one would read it. Here's the digest:

- **Baking pans:** Unless otherwise noted, I use sturdy but lightweight metal baking pans. As a general rule, I measure the inside dimensions across the top of the pan to determine its size. You'll need a variety of pan sizes and shapes if you want to bake everything in this book, but the one type no kitchen should be without is a rimmed baking sheet. The largest size that will fit in most home ovens is a 13 x 18-inch half-sheet pan, but you'll find quarter-sheets, which are about the size of a standard 9 x 13-inch baking dish, to be indispensable, too.
- **Bench scrapers and bowl scrapers:** Different shapes, different purposes.
- **Brushes:** I use these for greasing pans, dusting off flour, and applying egg wash.
- **Cake testers:** With practice, you can tell if a cake is done by the touch or the smell. Without it, insert a cake tester into the center to check that it comes out clean or with moist crumbs. I think bamboo skewers work better than the metal tools designed for this purpose. Go figure.
- **Measuring tools:** Aforementioned and debunked, but you still need something.
- **Mixers:** Most of the recipes in this book call for an electric mixer, and by that I mean a stand mixer, which is what I use in my kitchen. You can certainly use a handheld one if that's what you have available; the timings may be different (I haven't tried). There was once a time when everything was made by hand, too. Go for it—and show me your forearms after. Ten points!
- **Offset spatulas** in every shape and size, for measuring, spreading, moving, and swooping.
- **Rasp graters,** such as Microplanes, are the only way to zest.
- **Rolling pins:** In a pinch, I've used an empty bottle of wine for this purpose. I've used a full one, too. I would not recommend an open bottle.
- **Rubber spatulas,** various and sundry.
- **Rulers,** because we all have our obsessive compulsions.

- **Sieves,** both fine- and coarse-mesh, are indispensable for dusting finished cakes with confectioners' sugar and distributing flour into a delicate batter.
- **Silicone baking mats** are a fantastic reusable alternative to parchment paper and come in a variety of shapes and sizes.
- **Thermometers** can really take the guesswork out of baking. I use instant-read thermometers to check if yeasted doughs have cooked through and deep-fry or candy thermometers when making syrups. And—despite what I said earlier—an oven thermometer never hurt anyone.
- **Whisks:** Three of 'em. A balloon whisk for whipping, a narrow whisk for blending, and a small whisk for combining dry ingredients and beating eggs.
- **Wire cooling racks:** Thank you kindly.

A MORE RESPONSIBLE KITCHEN

If you're anything like me, you use more materials in the kitchen than in any other room in the house. From fresh produce to dish soap, it's a constant flow of new items coming in and going out. I've challenged myself to be a more conscientious cook by considering the environmental impact of my kitchen. I hope you'll join me. Here are some suggestions to get you started.

- **Shop light:** When you make purchases, look for products that are minimally packaged, avoiding plastics whenever possible. If you can purchase locally produced items, do.
- **Reuse:** Invest in sturdy containers that can be washed and reused rather than disposed of. Years ago, my grandmother taught me to rinse and reuse aluminum foil. I still do. Plastic bags, too.
- **Avoid:** There are some kitchen disposables we reach for out of habit, like plastic wrap and parchment paper, when new, reusable alternatives exist. Use beeswax wrap, which can be washed and reused, rather than plastic film whenever possible. Instead of using nonstick cooking spray, grease pans with Pan Goo (page 224) or line with reusable silicone baking mats. There are a handful of recipes in this book that call for parchment paper. I've found in those cases it's needed for a clean release; elsewhere, skip it.
- **Compost:** Food waste is the most easily recycled material on the planet. If your community has a composting program, participate. If not, talk to your neighbors about how you can start one.

Now, let's get to it.

CONSTANT CRAVINGS

For a moment I thought of calling this chapter "Brunch," because it was obvious and seemed relatable, but the fact is, I don't much care for brunch. Brunch is largely about waiting. My friends and I used to wait for a table at the local hot spot. Then we got older and switched to the decidedly uncool place next door. Eventually we waited there, too.

I'm far too boring to have brunch in restaurants now, but I still find myself waiting even when brunch is at home. Invariably, I get up too early and find myself overcaffeinated and needing a snack. Snacking, on the other hand, is something I excel at.

What I like about snacking is that there are no rules, and you can do it any time of day. I do some of my best snacking after sunset. These cakes are happy to oblige at any hour.

17	BANANA BREAD
19	BUTTERMILK RICOTTA AND PEACH CAKE
22	HONEY YUZU KASUTERA CAKE
26	BLACKBERRY BRETON
29	BANANA TIRAMISU
30	HAZELNUT PLUM SNACKING CAKE
33	SEMOLINA CAKE WITH FENNEL AND RAISINS
35	PEACH BOSTOCK
39	POACHED PEAR AND QUINCE CRUMB CAKE
41	BLUEBERRY GOOSEBERRY CRUMB CAKES
45	IRISH SODA BREAD
47	RASPBERRY TEA CAKE
50	MAPLE ORANGE CORNBREAD
53	APPLESAUCE CAKE
56	POLENTA POUND CAKE WITH SPICED MANDARINS
59	COCONUT APRICOT MACAROON CAKE
62	COCONUT POUND CAKE

BANANA BREAD

| MAKES 8 TO 10 SERVINGS | EASY |

The bananas and plantains for this recipe need to be soft, dark, and basically *mushade*, because that's when they are the sweetest and most full of flavor. The plantains, which are starchier than your typical banana, don't break down completely, forming little pockets of intense banana flavor scattered throughout the loaf.

Pan Goo (page 224), for greasing the pan		
large, very ripe, very mushy bananas	2	240 grams
large, very ripe, very soft sweet plantains	2	450 grams
granulated sugar	¾ cup	160 grams
all-purpose flour	1¼ cups	178 grams
coarse salt	1¼ teaspoons	3.8 grams
ground cinnamon	1 teaspoon	2.5 grams
baking soda	¾ teaspoon	4.5 grams
ground mace (see page 77)	1 pinch	1 pinch
unsalted butter, softened	4 tablespoons (½ stick)	57 grams
cream cheese, softened	½ cup (4 ounces)	113 grams
pure vanilla extract	2 teaspoons	10 milliliters
large eggs	2	2
chopped walnuts, lightly toasted (see page 18), optional	1 cup	100 grams

1. Preheat the oven to 350°F (180°C) with a rack in the center position. Brush a standard 8½ x 4½-inch loaf pan with Pan Goo.

2. In a large bowl, mash the bananas and plantains together until the bananas have almost totally disintegrated and the plantains have broken into pieces about the size of modest grapes. Add the sugar and continue mashing it all together until the sugar more or less dissolves.

Set this mixture aside to macerate for about 15 minutes.

3. In a small bowl, whisk together the flour, salt, cinnamon, baking soda, and mace.

4. In a small saucepan, melt the butter, then remove it from the heat. Using a rubber spatula, stir the cream cheese into the butter until it's mostly dissolved, then whisk to combine. Whisk in the vanilla and eggs, one at a time, until the

(continued)   **17**

mixture has lightened to the consistency of melted ice cream.

5. Stir the wet mixture into the banana mixture with a rubber spatula. Add the dry mixture and gently fold it all together as you might pancake batter, being careful not to overwork it or leave any dry pockets behind. Stir in the nuts, if using, and then pour the batter into the prepared pan. It will be almost completely full.

6. Bake the loaf until it's deep golden brown, springs back to the touch, and a cake tester inserted into the center comes out clean, 80 to 85 minutes.

7. Transfer the pan to a wire rack. Let the loaf rest in the pan for just about 15 minutes, then unmold it onto the rack until—here comes the hard part—it's completely cool.

STORAGE

You can probably keep the loaf in an airtight container for 4 or 5 days, but good luck with that.

FREEZING BANANAS

I never seem to have a shortage of well-browned bananas on hand, especially in the warmer months. If you want to save your bananas for a rainy day, do yourself a favor and peel them, then place in a freezer bag and freeze for up to 3 months. You can do the same with the plantains, just be sure to label them well so you can tell them apart. Thaw both before using.

TOASTING NUTS

Toast nuts by spreading in a single layer on a rimmed baking sheet. Bake in an oven preheated to 350°F (180°C) until fragrant, 8 to 10 minutes. Be careful not to let them burn.

BUTTERMILK RICOTTA AND PEACH CAKE

You could make this cake with store-bought ricotta, but it won't have the richness and complexity you get by making the ricotta yourself. All ricotta starts by acidifying milk to create curds; using buttermilk gives it a little culture. Not quite a degree in the arts, but an extended stay in a Tuscan village, maybe.

For best results, make the ricotta the day before baking and let it drain overnight in the refrigerator.

FOR THE BUTTERMILK RICOTTA

whole milk	2 cups	500 milliliters
heavy cream	1 cup	250 milliliters
buttermilk	¾ cup	187 milliliters
freshly squeezed lemon juice (from 1 lemon)	2 tablespoons	30 milliliters
coarse salt	1 teaspoon	3 grams

FOR THE CAKE

Pan Goo (page 224), for greasing the pan		
all-purpose flour	1¼ cups	178 grams
baking powder	1½ teaspoons	4.5 grams
coarse salt	1 teaspoon	3 grams
granulated sugar, divided	¾ cup plus 3 tablespoons	159 grams plus 40 grams
large eggs	2	2
unsalted butter, melted and cooled slightly	6 tablespoons (¾ stick)	85 grams
vanilla bean, split lengthwise and seeds scraped out	1	1
finely grated lemon zest (from 1 lemon)	1 teaspoon	2 grams
sliced firm-ripe peaches, ½ inch thick (from about 2 peaches)	1 cup	340 grams

(continued)

1. In a small saucepan, place the milk, cream, and buttermilk and heat over medium, stirring occasionally, until it reaches 200°F (93°C) on a candy thermometer and curds begin to form, about 15 minutes. Add the lemon juice and give it one last stir, then remove the pan from the heat and let it sit undisturbed for 30 minutes.

2. Stir in the salt. Drain the curds in the refrigerator overnight through a triple layer of cheesecloth set in a colander over a bowl. The cheese should be firm enough to just hold its shape and measure a little over 1 cup (about 250 grams) when it's ready.

3. Preheat the oven to 350°F (180°C) with a rack in the upper-third position. Brush a 9-inch springform pan with Pan Goo.

4. In a small bowl, whisk together the flour, baking powder, and salt.

5. In a large bowl, whisk the ricotta, ¾ cup (159 grams) of the sugar, the eggs, butter, vanilla seeds, and lemon zest until the mixture is rich and creamy. Stir the dry ingredients into the ricotta mixture until just combined, then scrape the batter into the pan.

6. Scatter the sliced peaches on top of the batter and sprinkle with the remaining 3 tablespoons (40 grams) of sugar.

7. Bake the cake until the edges are golden brown and a cake tester inserted into the center comes out with moist crumbs, about 45 minutes.

8. Transfer the pan to a wire rack. Allow the cake to cool for a few minutes before removing the collar from the pan. Serve warm or at room temperature.

STORAGE

This cake is best the day you make it, but leftovers can be covered and refrigerated for up to 2 days.

HONEY YUZU KASUTERA CAKE

| MAKES 8 TO 10 SERVINGS | ADVANCED | OVERNIGHT |
| SPECIAL EQUIPMENT: 10 X 5-INCH LOAF PAN |

Don't be fooled by its modest appearance. This pillow-soft sponge cake is an artful display of Japanese precision, and achieving perfection is an exercise in both mindfulness and obsession. It's worth the struggle. Kasutera cake has an ineffable springiness that comes from an unexpected ingredient: bread flour. Careful mixing keeps the cake meltingly tender with a perfectly even crumb. Lightly sweetened with honey and yuzu juice, this is a cake you would be hard-pressed to turn down at teatime.

Kasutera cakes, introduced to Japan from Portugal (where they are called castella cakes), are traditionally baked in wooden molds, but those are nearly impossible to come by outside of Japan. The wood insulates the cake as it cooks, which helps it remain perfectly flat as it rises. I find that baking in a low oven in conventional metal bakeware achieves a similar result, but I know purists will beg to differ. I see you, and I hear you.

vegetable oil, for brushing the pan		
honey	¼ cup	80 grams
yuzu juice (see page 24)	¼ cup	62 milliliters
bread flour	¾ cup	90 grams
dry milk powder	2 tablespoons	10 grams
large eggs, separated	4 whole, plus 2 yolks	4 whole, plus 2 yolks
granulated sugar	½ cup	106 grams
coarse salt	½ teaspoon	1.5 grams

1. Preheat the oven to 300°F (150°C) with a rack in the center position. Lightly brush a metal 10 x 5-inch loaf pan with oil. Line the pan with parchment paper running in both directions, leaving about 2 inches overhanging the long sides.

2. In a small saucepan, combine the honey and yuzu juice and stir over low heat just until the honey dissolves. Set aside.

3. Sift the bread flour and milk powder through a fine-mesh sieve two times.

4. The secret to a perfect kasutera cake is in the egg foam, as it's the sole leavening agent in the cake. Creating a perfectly even texture means avoiding uneven and large air bubbles at all costs. You do that by building the foam slowly and methodically: In a large pot, bring about 2 inches of water to a gentle simmer. In the heatproof bowl of an electric mixer, combine the egg whites, sugar, and salt. Set the bowl over the gently simmering water and whisk vigorously by hand until the sugar dissolves and the egg whites reach 140°F (60°C) on an instant-read thermometer, about 2 minutes.

5. Transfer the bowl to an electric mixer fitted with the whisk attachment. Whip on medium-low speed for 5 minutes.

6. Increase the mixer speed to medium and whip for 5 minutes more.

7. Increase the mixer speed to medium-high and whip until the meringue has quadrupled in volume, is firm but not dry, and the surface has a subtle sheen, about 5 minutes longer.

8. Remove the bowl from the mixer and continue assembling the cake by hand. Using a narrow whisk, stir the yolks into the meringue one at a time, using short, quick strokes to dissolve them into the whites, rather than incorporate more air. The meringue will soften as the yolks are added.

9. Drizzle about 2 tablespoons of the honey yuzu syrup over the foam and use short strokes to whisk the syrup into the batter. When the syrup disappears, add another 2 tablespoons and incorporate it in the same way.

10. Add the flour mixture slowly in 6 additions: Using a fine-mesh sieve, sift a light dusting over the batter and use a wide, flexible rubber

(continued) **23**

spatula to gently fold in the dry ingredients. This is the time to showcase your folding technique: Holding the blade of the spatula vertically, cut down through the center of the bowl and scoop up along the edge, gently turning the batter over itself. Rotate the bowl slightly after each stroke. Wait until the flour has almost completely disappeared before adding the next dose.

11. Fold the remaining syrup into the batter in two additions, taking care not to let it pool at the bottom of the bowl.

12. Much like making macarons, the final steps are meant to deflate the batter slightly, to remove any large bubbles, and to make sure the batter can flow easily. Continue folding gently for about 10 seconds, then firmly tap the bowl on the work surface two times. Let the bowl sit without being touched for 30 seconds.

13. Use the spatula to pop any large bubbles that rise to the surface. The batter should move like honey. If it's still too stiff, fold one or two more times to soften it further. Firmly tap the bowl on the work surface once more.

14. Pour the batter into the prepared pan extraordinarily slowly, letting it form a ribbon as it lands. Any remaining large bubbles will pop themselves as they stretch over the rim of the bowl. Drag a wooden skewer through the pan in a zigzag pattern in two directions to help spread the batter evenly and to all four corners. Firmly tap the pan on the work surface, bringing any remaining large bubbles up to the top.

15. Bake the cake until the surface is golden brown and springs back to the touch with a gentle squishing sound, about 50 minutes. A cake tester inserted into the center should come out clean or with very few crumbs.

16. Hold the cake pan about 1 foot above the work surface and drop it with great fanfare, knocking the wind out of it. (I had the wind knocked out of me once when I was a kid, and I'll never forget it.)

17. Wait about 30 seconds. The top of the cake will wrinkle slightly. Use a thin knife to loosen the corners of the cake from the pan where the parchment doesn't overlap. Using the overhanging parchment paper as handles, carefully lift the cake out of the pan and lay it top side down for about 45 seconds to smooth the top.

18. Flip the cake back over and slide it, parchment and all, into an extra-large (reusable) plastic bag. Seal the bag and refrigerate the cake for at least 12 hours, to allow the flavors to mature.

19. Bring the cake, still sealed in its bag, to room temperature before serving. Peel back the parchment and use a sharp serrated knife to trim the sides to create a perfectly rectangular loaf. Cut crosswise into slices about 1 inch thick.

STORAGE

Kasutera cake keeps remarkably well for 4 to 5 days, refrigerated in a plastic bag, but should be brought to room temperature and sliced just before serving.

YUZU JUICE

Yuzu is a special citrus and a much-loved ingredient in Japanese cuisine. You can find yuzu everything, from candies to marmalade and even hot sauces. It's an unmistakable flavor: lemony, sure, but with floral notes not unlike bergamot and a sweetness that comes from its cousin the mandarin orange. Fresh yuzu is difficult, but not impossible, to find outside of Japan; bottled juice is readily available at Japanese markets and online. Make sure to pick one that is 100 percent yuzu juice for the best flavor.

Eggs and sugar

whipped together

Make meringues

in decent weather

On stormy days

it's shaky legs

Better to make

scrambled eggs

BLACKBERRY BRETON

| MAKES 8 TO 10 SERVINGS | EASY | SPECIAL EQUIPMENT: 9-INCH TART PAN |

When you go to spread this cake batter into the pan, you might wonder if you've made enough. It forms a thin layer, just enough to envelop the berries as it bakes, creating pockets of deep purple. This is a cake with some chew—dense and satisfying in small slices, but not so sweet that you can't have many. Serve warm for a dose of summer at any time.

all-purpose flour	½ cup	71 grams
finely ground almond flour (see opposite)	½ cup	50 grams
baking powder	1 teaspoon	3 grams
coarse salt	¼ teaspoon	0.8 gram
unsalted butter, softened	4 tablespoons (½ stick)	57 grams
granulated sugar	½ cup	106 grams
large eggs	2	2
almond extract	½ teaspoon	2.5 milliliters
fresh blackberries	1 generous cup	155 grams

1. Dig around in your cabinet for a 9-inch tart pan with a removable bottom. Don't bother greasing it. Preheat the oven to 350°F (180°C) with a rack in the center position.

2. In a small bowl, whisk together both flours, the baking powder, and salt. Set aside.

3. Using an electric mixer fitted with the paddle attachment, beat the butter and sugar together until they form a sparkly sort of a paste, then add the eggs one at a time, beating for a minute or so after each. Add the almond extract and mix well. Scrape down the sides of the bowl and scrape off the beater; the mixture will be borderline soupy until you add the dry ingredients, which you can go ahead and do now in one fell swoop.

4. Mix on low speed until just combined, about 30 seconds. Scrape the batter into the pan and spread it to the edges using a small offset spatula. It's a piddling little bit of batter, so try not to leave a speck behind.

5. Scatter the blackberries evenly over the surface, leaving about ½ inch of space between them. Set the tart pan on a rimmed baking sheet, lest there be any mess, and scoot it into the oven.

6. Bake for about 28 minutes, until the cake has risen around the berries, is golden brown around the edges, and springs back nicely to the touch.

7. Transfer the pan to a wire rack to cool. Don't even think about trying to pop the cake out of the pan until it has cooled completely.

STORAGE

You can keep the cake in an airtight container at room temperature for a day or so.

ALMOND FLOUR

Almond flour is simply made by grinding almonds to a fine meal. These days it's quite easy to find in stores, but you can make it at home by pulsing sliced almonds in the food processor until finely ground. Be careful to stop before the flour becomes almond butter.

BANANA TIRAMISU

| MAKES 12 TO 16 SERVINGS | EASY |

Tiramisu is Italian for "pick me up," and what better way to lift your spirits than with chocolate, coffee, and booze? I've gone rogue and filled mine with bananas for extra flair—call it banana pudding if you must, but at least say it in Italian.

You can get away with store-bought ladyfingers, if you insist.

large ripe bananas, divided	3 to 4	360 to 480 grams
granulated sugar, divided	3 tablespoons	39 grams
mascarpone cheese	1 cup	226 grams
heavy cream	1 cup	250 milliliters
freshly brewed strong coffee or espresso, cooled slightly	1 cup	250 milliliters
dark rum, optional (but also not?)	2 glugs	2 glugs
crisp Ladyfingers (page 227), baked and cooled	20-ish	20-ish
unsweetened cocoa powder, preferably Dutch-processed, divided	4 teaspoons	6 grams

1. In a large bowl, mash the two ripest bananas with 2 tablespoons (26 grams) of the sugar, using a potato masher or fork, until very few lumps remain. Mash in the mascarpone.

2. In another large bowl, whip the cream and remaining 1 tablespoon (13 grams) of sugar until stiff peaks form. You can do it by hand; think how nice your forearms will be. Gently fold the whipped cream into the banana mixture.

3. In a shallow bowl, stir together the coffee and rum, if using.

4. Quickly dip some of the ladyfingers in the spiked coffee and use them to line the bottom of an 8 x 2-inch square baking dish, breaking them as needed to form an even layer. It should take about 10. Evenly spread half the banana cream over the ladyfingers. Thinly slice the remaining banana and arrange the slices neatly over the cream, then generously dust everything with 2 teaspoons (3 grams) of the cocoa powder. Repeat the process with the remaining ladyfingers and banana cream.

5. Chill the tiramisu, covered, for at least 3 hours (or up to 2 days) before serving, to allow time for the flavors to harmonize. Dust with the remaining 2 teaspoons (3 grams) of cocoa powder just before serving generous scoops.

STORAGE

This will keep in the refrigerator, covered, for up to 2 days.

HAZELNUT PLUM SNACKING CAKE

| MAKES 12 TO 14 SERVINGS | EASY |
| SPECIAL EQUIPMENT: 9-INCH SPRINGFORM PAN |

Here in New York, Italian plums arrive toward the end of the summer, a bittersweet reminder of what's to come. I don't much mind; New York is nicest in the fall. I can already see the light changing from platinum to gold, and this morning there was a chill in the air—but it could have been the poltergeist.

That's the other thing I like about the fall: It's spooky. I like to be scared because otherwise I'm just nervous, and I find strangers are more generous with people they think have reason to be neurotic. Louisa is good for that. She's the poltergeist. I could loan her to you if you'd like. She gets along with almost anyone and mostly just eats socks.

Pan Goo (page 224), for greasing the pan		
raw hazelnuts	1 cup	128 grams
all-purpose flour	¾ cup	107 grams
granulated sugar	⅔ cup	141 grams
baking powder	1¼ teaspoons	3.8 grams
coarse salt	½ teaspoon	1.5 grams
unsalted butter, cut into ½-inch pieces	6 tablespoons (¾ stick)	85 grams
large eggs	3	3
fresh small Italian prune plums, halved and pitted	7 (about 14 ounces total)	397 grams

1. Preheat the oven to 350°F (180°C) with a rack in the center position. Brush a 9-inch springform pan with Pan Goo and set aside.
2. Place the hazelnuts on a rimmed baking sheet and roast for 12 to 14 minutes, until the skins crack and the nuts are golden brown.
3. Immediately roll the nuts onto a clean kitchen towel and gather the corners, forming a purse that, were you a hobo, you might attach to a stick. Before you ride off in a boxcar, consider this: They've come a long way with high-speed trains.

4. Rub the nuts,* using the towel to help dislodge as many of the skins as can easily be done; the rest will add color to the batter. Cool slightly, then transfer to the bowl of a food processor, leaving the skins behind.
5. Pulse the hazelnuts until just finely ground, 30 to 45 seconds. Add the flour, sugar, baking powder, and salt and pulse until well combined.

* The address to complain to is: William Morrow Cookbooks, c/o HarperCollins Publishers, 195 Broadway, New York, NY 10007.

Add the butter and continue pulsing until the mixture is the texture of wet sand. With the food processor running, add the eggs through the feed tube, one at a time, processing until a rich batter forms, about another minute or so. Scrape the batter into the prepared pan and smooth the top with an offset spatula. Arrange the plums skin side up on top of the batter.

6. Bake the cake for about 35 minutes, until the batter has bubbled over the plums, the cake is golden brown and springs back to the touch, and a cake tester inserted into the center comes out clean.

7. Transfer the pan to a wire rack. Allow the cake to cool for about 10 minutes before removing the collar to let the cake cool completely on the rack.

STORAGE

Kept in an airtight container at room temperature, the cake will be just as good (or maybe even better) the next day, or for up to 3 days.

SEMOLINA CAKE WITH FENNEL AND RAISINS

| MAKES 10 TO 12 SERVINGS | EASY |

There's nothing quite like semolina. The coarse texture of the flour makes this cake at once dense and crumbly, not unlike a corn muffin, but with just a little more bite. The combination of fennel and orange adds an Italian vibe, but, like all semolina cakes, its true home is in the Eastern Mediterranean, where yogurt reigns supreme. As the cake cools, it will soak up the raisin and orange syrup like a sponge. Despite this you'll find it just a tad sweet. A simple end to a perfect evening. A perfect start to a simple day.

FOR THE CAKE

unsalted butter, melted and cooled slightly, plus more for greasing the pan	¾ cup (1½ sticks)	170 grams
semolina flour, plus more for dusting the pan	2½ cups	390 grams
golden raisins, preferably hunza	1 cup	160 grams
boiling water	¾ cup	187 milliliters
baking powder	2½ teaspoons	7.5 grams
freshly ground cardamom (see page 11)	½ teaspoon	1 gram
ground fennel seeds	½ teaspoon	1 gram
coarse salt	½ teaspoon	1.5 grams
plain, whole-milk yogurt (not Greek-style)	1½ cups	345 grams
granulated sugar	1 cup	212 grams
large eggs	1 whole, plus 1 yolk	1 whole, plus 1 yolk
finely grated orange zest (from 1 orange)	2 teaspoons	4 grams

FOR THE SYRUP

granulated sugar	½ cup	106 grams
fennel seeds	3 tablespoons	18 grams
coarse salt	1 pinch	1 pinch
freshly squeezed orange juice (from 1 orange)	¼ cup	60 milliliters

(continued)

1. Preheat the oven to 350°F (180°C). Brush a 10 x 2-inch round cake pan with melted butter. Dust with semolina flour, turning the pan to coat, and tap out the excess.

2. In a small bowl, combine the raisins with the boiling water and let them soak for about 15 minutes while you prepare the rest of the cake.

3. In a medium bowl, whisk together the semolina, baking powder, cardamom, ground fennel, and salt. Set aside.

4. In a large bowl, whisk together the yogurt, sugar, egg, yolk, and zest. Whisk in the melted butter a little at a time, until a creamy mixture is formed. Stir the dry ingredients into the yogurt mixture using a wooden spoon or a rubber spatula until they are just combined and no dry pockets remain.

5. Drain the raisins, reserving the soaking liquid— there should be about ½ cup (125 milliliters). Fold the raisins into the batter and scrape it into the prepared pan.

6. Bake the cake until it's firm to the touch and golden around the edges, about 40 minutes.

7. Make the syrup while the cake is in the oven. In a small saucepan, combine the reserved raisin soaking liquid with the sugar, fennel seeds, and salt. Bring to a boil over medium heat and cook until the fennel is fragrant, 1 to 2 minutes. Remove from the heat and stir in the orange juice.

8. When the cake is done baking, remove it from the oven and let it cool in the pan for 10 minutes. Run a knife around the edge and invert the cake onto a serving platter. Strain the syrup over the cake through a mesh sieve and allow it to cool completely. Serve today or tomorrow—morning, noon, or night.

STORAGE

Store the cake at room temperature, lightly covered, for up to 3 days.

A DOLLOP WILL DO IT

I love this cake on its own, but you can dress it up with lightly sweetened yogurt and candied fennel seeds, available at specialty spice stores, as a garnish.

PEACH BOSTOCK

| MAKES 8 SERVINGS | EASY |

The bread used for bostock should be oven-dried, which is not at all the same as stale. Stale bread is hard. Dry bread is crisp, with a marked propensity to absorb whatever you throw at it. Use the best brioche you can find in this recipe. Use the best peaches you can find, too.

FOR THE SYRUP

granulated sugar	⅓ cup	71 grams
peaches, pitted and coarsely chopped	2 (about 12 ounces total)	340 grams
small lemongrass stalk, trimmed and bruised	1	35 grams

FOR THE ALMOND CREAM

almond paste (not marzipan)	½ cup	140 grams
granulated sugar	¼ cup	53 grams
large egg	1	1
all-purpose flour	¼ cup	36 grams
bourbon, optional	2 tablespoons	30 milliliters
unsalted butter, softened	4 tablespoons (½ stick)	57 grams
coarse salt	1 pinch	1 pinch

FOR ASSEMBLY

thick slices brioche	8 (about 14 ounces total)	about 400 grams
firm-ripe peaches, thinly sliced	2 (about 12 ounces total)	340 grams
confectioners' sugar, for serving		

(continued)

1. In a small saucepan, combine the granulated sugar, peaches, lemongrass, and ¾ cup (187 milliliters) water. Bring to a boil over high heat, stirring until the sugar dissolves, about 2 minutes. Remove from the heat and mash the peach and lemongrass until they're unrecognizable, then let the syrup sit until it's cool. Strain through a coarse-mesh sieve, pressing on the solids to squeeze out every last bit of flavor. You can store the syrup in the refrigerator for a day or two before using.

2. To make the almond cream, combine the almond paste, granulated sugar, egg, flour, and bourbon (please) in the bowl of an electric mixer. Beat on medium speed until smooth, then add the butter and a pinch of salt. Continue beating until very light and very fluffy. You can refrigerate the almond cream overnight, but make sure to bring it to room temperature before assembling the bostock.

3. Preheat the oven to 275°F (140°C) with a rack in the center position.

4. Place the brioche slices on a 13 x 18-inch rimmed baking sheet and bake until they're very dry and just beginning to brown, about 30 minutes, flipping the bread halfway so they dry evenly. Let the slices cool a few minutes until they're easy to handle, or cool completely and store in an airtight container at room temperature overnight.

5. Increase the oven temperature to 350°F (180°C). Line a 13 x 18-inch rimmed baking sheet with a reusable nonstick silicone baking mat, or use parchment paper if you are just out of options. Brush the brioche slices with the syrup, coating both sides, until they feel heavy in your hands. Arrange the soaked slices on the baking sheet and spread each with about 3 tablespoons of almond cream. Arrange 3 or 4 peach slices on each in a single layer on top of the almond cream.

6. Bake until the almond cream has puffed and browned on the edges, 25 to 30 minutes.

7. Remove from the oven and allow the bostock to cool slightly before dusting with confectioners' sugar. Serve warm.

STORAGE

Bostock is best the day you bake it.

POACHED PEAR AND QUINCE CRUMB CAKE

| MAKES ABOUT 15 SERVINGS | INTERMEDIATE | OVERNIGHT |

Cubes of membrillo and poached pears stud this tender cake, heavy on the crumb topping, which I think we can all agree is the main event. Poaching the pears the night before baking will reward you with the flavor boost that can only come from taking your time—and will make for one less thing to worry about on bake day.

FOR THE POACHED PEARS

small Bosc pears, peeled, cored, and quartered	2	352 grams
firmly packed light brown sugar	½ cup	106 grams
fresh ginger, thinly sliced	2 inches	30 grams
green cardamom pods, cracked	7	7

FOR THE CRUMB TOPPING

all-purpose flour	1⅓ cups	189 grams
granulated sugar	⅔ cup	141 grams
coarse salt	½ teaspoon	1.5 grams
freshly ground cardamom (see page 11)	½ teaspoon	1 gram
unsalted butter, cut into ½-inch pieces and softened	½ cup (1 stick)	113 grams

FOR THE CAKE AND ASSEMBLY

Pan Goo (page 224), for greasing the pan		
all-purpose flour	1½ cups	213 grams
granulated sugar	1 cup	212 grams
baking powder	1½ teaspoons	4.5 grams
coarse salt	½ teaspoon	1.5 grams
unsalted butter, cut into ½-inch pieces and softened	½ cup (1 stick)	113 grams
large eggs	2	2
whole milk	½ cup	125 milliliters
pure vanilla extract	2 teaspoons	10 milliliters
membrillo (quince paste), cut into ½-inch cubes	½ cup	100 grams

(continued)

1. In a small saucepan, place the pears along with the light brown sugar, ginger, and cardamom pods. Add enough water so that the pears just begin to float—about 2 cups (500 milliliters) should do it. Set the pan over medium heat and bring to a low simmer with the lid askew just enough to drive your OCD wild. Simmer gently for 15 to 20 minutes, until the pears feel tender when pierced with a knife but are not falling apart. Let them cool completely in the syrup, then refrigerate overnight or up to 3 days.

2. While you're at it, you might as well make the crumb topping. In a medium bowl, whisk together the flour, granulated sugar, salt, and cardamom. Add the butter, working it into the flour mixture with your hands, until the mixture forms clumps when you squeeze it firmly. Refrigerate for at least 1 hour or overnight.

3. Preheat the oven to 350°F (180°C) with a rack in the center position. Line the bottom and two long sides of a 9 x 13 x 2-inch cake pan with a sheet of parchment paper, leaving about 2 inches overhanging the sides. Brush with Pan Goo. (Skip the parchment if you're okay serving the cake directly out of the pan.)

4. Pull the pears out of the syrup and shake off the excess, then slice them the long way into scant ½-inch-thick pieces. Set aside.

5. In the bowl of an electric mixer fitted with the paddle attachment, stir together the flour, granulated sugar, baking powder, and salt. Add the butter and beat on medium speed until it's completely incorporated and the mixture becomes sandy, 2 to 3 minutes.

6. Meanwhile, in a large measuring cup, lightly beat the eggs, milk, and vanilla.

7. Reduce the mixer speed to low and add the milk mixture. When all of the dry ingredients have been moistened, increase the speed to medium-high and beat until the batter is smooth and voluminous, about 2 minutes longer. Scrape down the sides of the bowl to make sure no dry bits are stuck at the bottom.

8. Pour the batter into the prepared pan and spread to the edges with a small offset spatula. Evenly scatter the pear slices and cubes of membrillo over the batter, then generously cover everything with glorious clumps of crumb topping.

9. Bake the until the cake springs back to the touch and a cake tester inserted into the center comes out clean, about 50 minutes.

10. Remove the pan from the oven. Allow the cake to cool completely in the pan. Use the overhanging parchment paper as handles to lift the cake out of the pan to serve, or slice and serve it right from the pan. Either way it's delicious.

STORAGE

The cake will still be good tomorrow, if you keep it covered at room temperature.

BLUEBERRY GOOSEBERRY CRUMB CAKES

| MAKES 2 CAKES, OR 14 TO 16 SERVINGS | EASY |

Fresh gooseberries can be hard to find if you don't have a good farmers' market nearby, but they freeze well. Pairing them with blueberries is as delectable as it is fun to say, and the balanced, tart sweetness embodies summer. These impressive loaves make great gifts, so the recipe makes two: one for you and one for me.

FOR THE CRUMB TOPPING

all-purpose flour	¾ cup	107 grams
old-fashioned oats	¾ cup	69 grams
firmly packed light brown sugar	¾ cup	159 grams
coarse salt	¾ teaspoon	2.3 grams
freshly ground cardamom (see page 11)	½ teaspoon	1 gram
unsalted butter, softened	6 tablespoons (¾ stick)	85 grams

FOR THE CAKES

Pan Goo (page 224), for greasing the pans		
cake flour, divided	3 cups plus 2 tablespoons	339 grams plus 14 grams
coarse salt	1 teaspoon	3 grams
baking powder	1 teaspoon	3 grams
baking soda	½ teaspoon	3 grams
blueberries	1¼ cups	175 grams
gooseberries, stems and flowers removed (thawed, if frozen)	1¼ cups	215 grams
unsalted butter, softened	1 cup (2 sticks)	226 grams
granulated sugar	1½ cups	318 grams
finely grated lemon zest (from 1 lemon)	1 teaspoon	2 grams
large eggs	4	4
sour cream	1 cup	244 grams
pure vanilla extract	1 tablespoon	15 milliliters

(continued)

blueberries	¼ cup	35 grams
gooseberries, stems and flowers removed	¼ cup	43 grams
unsalted butter	1 tablespoon	14 grams
confectioners' sugar	½ cup	57 grams

1. For the crumb topping: In a medium bowl, whisk together the all-purpose flour, oats, light brown sugar, salt, and cardamom. Add the butter and work it into the dry ingredients with your fingers until all the flour has been moistened and the mixture clumps together when you squeeze it in your delicate little fists. Refrigerate while you make the cake batter.

2. Preheat the oven to 350°F (180°C) with a rack in the center position. Generously brush two standard 8½ x 4½-inch loaf pans with Pan Goo.

3. In a medium bowl, whisk together 3 cups (339 grams) of the cake flour, the salt, baking powder, and baking soda. Set aside.

4. In another medium bowl, toss the blueberries and gooseberries with the remaining 2 tablespoons (14 grams) of cake flour. Set aside.

5. In the bowl of an electric mixer fitted with the paddle attachment, beat the butter, granulated sugar, and lemon zest on medium speed until well combined, about 2 minutes. Scrape down the sides of the bowl and add the eggs one at a time, beating well after each addition. Beat on medium-high speed for another minute or so, until the mixture is very light and fluffy. Add the sour cream and vanilla and mix thoroughly on medium speed. The batter may appear a little broken at this point.

6. With the mixer running on low speed, slowly add the dry ingredients. Increase the speed to medium and beat for about 30 seconds to make a thick, rich batter. Stir in the floured berries by hand.

7. Spoon about half of the batter into the prepared pans, filling each pan about halfway. Sprinkle each with about ¼ cup of the crumb topping, then divide the rest of the cake batter between the two pans and strew with the remaining crumble.

8. Bake the cakes for about 70 minutes, until a cake tester inserted into the centers comes out clean, tenting with foil if they darken too quickly.

9. Transfer the pans to a wire rack and allow the cakes to cool for about 1 hour before unmolding onto the rack to cool completely.

10. Make the glaze: In a small saucepan, combine the blueberries, gooseberries, and butter. Cook over medium heat, mashing the berries with a wooden spoon until they burst and the juice thickens and turns a vibrant purple, about 5 minutes. Press the mixture through a coarse-mesh sieve, discarding the solids. Stir in the confectioners' sugar. Adjust the consistency with a little water or extra sugar until the glaze coats the back of a spoon. Drizzle over the cakes and let stand until the glaze sets, about 10 minutes.

STORAGE

Store at room temperature in an airtight container for a few days or cover and refrigerate for to up to 1 week.

MAKING DO

If you don't have gooseberries, you can still make a delicious cake by doubling the blueberries in this recipe.

IRISH SODA BREAD

| MAKES 8 SERVINGS | EASY |

I'd like to visit Ireland because of its rampant population of mischievous small men—imagine the luxury of always having a leprechaun to blame. Add to that the complete absence of snakes and it's a wonder that I haven't settled down on the Emerald Isle.

For the time being this soda bread will have to suffice. Like a good leprechaun, it's flaky, tender, and laden with golden butter.

coarsely grated unpeeled tart apple (from 1 large apple)	about 1 cup	145 grams
dried currants	⅔ cup	92 grams
whiskey (preferably Irish)	2 tablespoons	30 milliliters
all-purpose flour	4 cups	568 grams
granulated sugar	⅓ cup	71 grams
caraway seeds	1 tablespoon	10 grams
coarse salt	1½ teaspoons	4.5 grams
baking soda	1 teaspoon	6 grams
large egg	1	1
buttermilk	about ⅓ cup	about 83 milliliters
cider vinegar	3 tablespoons	45 milliliters
unsalted butter, cold and cut into ½-inch pieces	10 tablespoons (1¼ sticks)	141 grams
salted cultured butter, softened, for serving		

1. Preheat the oven to 350°F (180°C) with a rack in the center position. Line a 13 x 18-inch rimmed baking sheet with a silicone baking mat or parchment paper.

2. In a medium bowl, toss the grated apple with the currants and whiskey. Let them macerate for about 10 minutes while you prepare the rest of the ingredients.

3. In a large bowl, whisk together the flour, sugar, caraway seeds, salt, and baking soda. Set aside.

4. In a liquid measuring cup, lightly beat the egg and add enough buttermilk to equal ⅔ cup (166 milliliters). Add the cider vinegar and whisk to combine. Set aside.

(continued)

5. Using a pastry blender or, let's be honest, your hands, rub the unsalted butter pieces into the flour mixture until it feels a little bit like lentils, but mostly like a bowl of flour. Add the soaked apple, currants, and any remaining liquid to the bowl and toss through the flour mixture with your hands, breaking up the clumps of fruit and distributing evenly throughout.

6. Make a well in the center of the bowl and pour in the buttermilk mixture. Use a wooden spoon to stir the dry ingredients into the wet until it just comes together as a soft dough. There will be some dry bits that accumulate at the bottom of the bowl. Squeeze the dough into a ball, gently working the dry bits into the wet. Try not to knead the dough so much as consolidate it; the less you handle it the better.

7. Gather the dough ball in your hands and place it in the center of the prepared baking sheet. Press the ball into a disc that's about 6 inches across and use a sharp knife to score an X across the top, cutting about 1 inch deep.

8. Bake the soda bread until it's puffy and golden brown and a cake tester inserted into the center comes out with moist crumbs, about 50 minutes.

9. Transfer the baking sheet to a wire rack. Allow the bread to cool on the baking sheet for about 15 minutes, then transfer it to the rack to cool completely. Serve with softened cultured butter, warm or at room temperature.

STORAGE

Don't plan on keeping this one around very long. It's really best the day it's baked.

RASPBERRY TEA CAKE

| MAKES 8 TO 10 SERVINGS | EASY |

In my book, and I guess I mean that quite literally, tea cakes are delicate and tender with a compact crumb. Sort of like if pound cake spent a weekend watching *Room with a View* and dreamed of being younger and mildly rebellious.

This one is elegant enough with its pink glaze and pockets of berries, but it packs a secret punch—a hint of black pepper to whisk away those midafternoon blues.

FOR THE CAKE

Pan Goo (page 224), for greasing the pan		
cake flour, divided	1½ cups plus 1 tablespoon	170 grams plus 7 grams
finely ground black pepper	1 teaspoon	2 grams
coarse salt	½ teaspoon	1.5 grams
baking powder	½ teaspoon	1.5 grams
baking soda	¼ teaspoon	1.5 grams
unsalted butter, softened	½ cup (1 stick)	113 grams
granulated sugar	¾ cup	159 grams
pure vanilla extract	2 teaspoons	10 milliliters
finely grated lemon zest (from 1 lemon)	1 teaspoon	2 grams
large eggs	2	2
buttermilk	½ cup	125 milliliters
fresh raspberries, divided	6 ounces (about 1¼ cups)	170 grams

FOR THE GLAZE AND FINISHING

confectioners' sugar	½ cup	56 grams
coarse salt	1 pinch	1 pinch
sugared lemon peel (see page 49), for garnish		

(continued)

1. Preheat the oven to 350°F (180°C) with a rack in the center position. Generously brush a standard 8½ x 4½-inch loaf pan with Pan Goo.

2. In a small bowl, whisk together the 1½ cups (170 grams) cake flour, the pepper, salt, baking powder, and baking soda. Set aside.

3. In the bowl of an electric mixer fitted with the paddle attachment, beat the butter, granulated sugar, vanilla, and lemon zest on medium speed until it sparkles, about 1 minute. Add the eggs one at a time, scraping down the sides of the bowl before, during, meanwhile, and after. It's a lot of scraping you should be doing.

4. Add about one third of the flour mixture and stir on low speed until almost no dry patches remain, then slowly stream in about half the buttermilk. Add another third of the dry ingredients, followed by the remaining buttermilk and the last of the dry, mixing well, but not aggressively, after each addition.

5. Increase the mixer speed to high and beat well for 1 minute.

6. Set 5 or 6 raspberries aside for the glaze. Cut the rest into halves and thirds and gently toss with the remaining 1 tablespoon (7 grams) of cake flour. Stir about two thirds of the coated raspberries into the batter by hand. Some will break down, but you won't. Scrape the batter into the prepared pan and smooth out the top. Scatter the remaining third of the berries over the top of the batter. Give the pan a firm tap on the counter to release any large air bubbles.

7. Bake until the cake is golden brown and a cake tester inserted into the center comes out clean, about 70 minutes.

8. Transfer the pan to a wire rack. Let the cake rest in the pan for 10 minutes, then carefully unmold onto the rack to cool completely.

9. To make the glaze, muddle the reserved raspberries with the confectioners' sugar and salt in a small bowl. Adjust the consistency by adding water, drop by drop, until it moves easily without being runny. Spread the glaze on top of the cake and garnish with sugared lemon peel. Don't wait too long before serving.

STORAGE

The cake will last for about 3 days at room temperature in an airtight container.

SUGARED LEMON PEEL

The best-looking lemon peel comes from a bartender's stripper—not a stripper's bartender—which makes long, thin curls rather than the shavings you get from a typical grater. Toss the peel with a little sugar and let it air dry for 30 minutes or so before using as garnish, or store in an airtight container at room temperature for up to 1 month.

MAPLE ORANGE CORNBREAD

Each November, an email exchange between my mother and me resurfaces. The conversation goes back more than ten years, which is a testament to both our forgetfulness and the resilience of modern technology. The subject: cornbread, and how. Each year the recipe is tweaked and changed, adapted and scaled. No more. I have put it down in ink now, for my mom and yours.

FOR THE CORNBREAD

Pan Goo (page 224), for greasing the pan		
all-purpose flour	2 cups	284 grams
stone-ground cornmeal	1 cup	115 grams
coarse salt	1½ teaspoons	4.5 grams
baking powder	1 teaspoon	3 grams
baking soda	½ teaspoon	3 grams
finely grated orange zest (from 1 orange)	2 teaspoons	4 grams
granulated sugar	¾ cup	159 grams
large eggs	3	3
pure maple syrup, preferably dark and robust	¼ cup	84 grams
unsalted butter, melted and cooled	½ cup (1 stick)	113 grams
buttermilk, room temperature	1 cup	250 milliliters

FOR THE GLAZE

freshly squeezed orange juice	¼ cup	62 milliliters
pure maple syrup, preferably dark and robust	2 tablespoons	42 grams
unsalted butter	1 tablespoon	14 grams
coarse salt	1 pinch	1 pinch

(continued)

FRUIT CAKE

1. Preheat the oven to 350°F (180°C) with a rack in the center position. Brush a 9 x 2-inch square cake pan with Pan Goo.

2. In a large bowl, whisk together the flour, cornmeal, salt, baking powder, and baking soda and set aside.

3. In a medium bowl, use your fingers to rub the orange zest into the sugar, releasing all the fragrant oils. Whisk the eggs into the sugar one at a time until well combined. Slowly whisk in the maple syrup, followed by the melted butter. Finally, whisk in the buttermilk. The mixture should be very smooth.

4. Make a well in the center of the flour mixture and pour in the wet ingredients. Use a rubber spatula or a wooden spoon to gently stir the dry ingredients into the wet as you would pancake batter. Be careful not to overmix or the cake will become tough; leave some lumps of love. Scrape the batter into the prepared pan.

5. Bake until the top springs back when gently pressed and a cake tester inserted into the center comes out with moist crumbs, 35 to 40 minutes.

6. Make the glaze while the cake is in the oven: In a small saucepan, combine the orange juice, maple syrup, butter, and salt. Set over medium heat and cook, stirring occasionally, until the mixture boils. Continue boiling without stirring for 2 minutes, then remove the pan from the heat.

7. Transfer the cake pan to a wire rack. Brush the top of the cornbread with the maple orange glaze as soon as it comes out of the oven, then let it cool completely in the pan. Serve warm or at room temperature.

STORAGE

Cornbread is really best eaten the day it's made but will keep reasonably well at room temperature in an airtight container for up to 3 days.

APPLESAUCE CAKE

| MAKES 12 TO 16 SERVINGS | EASY |
| SPECIAL EQUIPMENT: 10-CUP BUNDT PAN, CHEESECLOTH |

My parents gave me an apple tree for my eighth birthday. I wish I could tell you how crisp and delicious those apples were, but the damn thing never grew any. We didn't know it takes two trees to tango. So, we picked our apples from others' orchards, lugging too-full satchels over undulating hills, searching first for the perfect tree, later for the car or any sign of civilization. A woodsman would find us eventually, collapsed in the shade, and show us how to drink from the water trapped in the foliage. I guess we live here now, we'd say. The parking lot couldn't have been more than a few feet away, but it was impossible to know.

When choosing an apple, reach for something flavorful that won't break down in the oven, since this batter is already laden with applesauce. The cake is best with something tart and acidic—not unlike a Granny Smith, but I think you can do better. If you need advice, ask the woodsman.

FOR THE CAKE

Pan Goo (page 224), for greasing the pan		
all-purpose flour	2¾ cups	391 grams
baking powder	2¾ teaspoons	8.3 grams
ground cinnamon	2 teaspoons	5 grams
coarse salt	1½ teaspoons	4.5 grams
freshly grated nutmeg (see page 12)	15 seconds (about ¾ teaspoon)	1.5 grams
unsalted butter, softened	10 tablespoons (1¼ sticks)	141 grams
firmly packed dark brown sugar	1 cup	212 grams
granulated sugar	½ cup	106 grams
large eggs	4	4
Applesauce (page 243 or store-bought unsweetened)	2 cups	488 grams
cider vinegar	2 tablespoons	30 milliliters
large apple, peeled, cored, and roughly chopped into ¼-inch pieces	1	145 grams
walnuts, broken into halves and pieces	1½ cups	153 grams

(continued)

confectioners' sugar	¾ cup	85 grams
freshly grated ginger	1 tablespoon	15 grams
bourbon, optional	1 tablespoon	15 milliliters
coarse salt	1 pinch	1 pinch

1. Preheat the oven to 350°F (180°C) with a rack in the lower-third position. Generously brush a 10-cup (9-inch-diameter) Bundt pan with Pan Goo, making sure you cover every nook and cranny.

2. In a medium bowl, whisk together the flour, baking powder, cinnamon, salt, and nutmeg. Set aside.

3. In the bowl of an electric mixer fitted with the paddle attachment, beat the butter, dark brown sugar, and granulated sugar on medium speed until well combined, about 3 minutes. Add the eggs one at a time, stopping to scrape down the sides of the bowl occasionally. When all the eggs have been incorporated, beat on medium-high speed for about 30 seconds, until the mixture is luxuriously soft and smooth.

4. Stop the mixer and add about half the dry ingredients. Mix on low speed until almost everything has been moistened, then stir in the applesauce and cider vinegar. Add the remaining dry ingredients and stir by hand until the mixture forms a smooth, thick batter. Stir in the chopped apple and walnuts and spoon the batter into the prepared pan.

5. Bake until the cake is firm and springs back to the touch and a cake tester inserted into the center comes out clean, about 65 minutes.

6. Transfer the pan to a wire rack. Let the cake rest in the pan for 20 minutes, then invert onto the rack to cool completely, about 40 minutes longer.

7. When the cake has cooled, make the glaze by placing the confectioners' sugar in a medium bowl. Squeeze the ginger over the sugar through a double layer of cheesecloth or sturdy paper towel, extracting as much juice as possible, then add the bourbon (if using) and salt. Stir everything together with a small whisk or a rubber spatula, adding water by the teaspoon, until the mixture coats the back of a spoon.

8. Drizzle the glaze over the cooled cake and allow it to set at room temperature before serving.

STORAGE

This cake keeps remarkably well, lightly covered at room temperature, for close to 1 week.

POLENTA POUND CAKE WITH SPICED MANDARINS

| MAKES 8 TO 10 SERVINGS | EASY |

If you wanted to, you could plate this in individual servings elegant enough for the nicest restaurant in town, but you absolutely do not have to.

FOR THE POLENTA POUND CAKE

Pan Goo (page 224), for greasing the pan		
all-purpose flour	1¾ cups	249 grams
baking powder	1¾ teaspoons	5.3 grams
coarse salt	½ teaspoon	1.5 grams
quick-cooking (but not instant) polenta, divided	2 tablespoons plus ¼ cup	22 grams plus 44 grams
orange liqueur, such as Triple Sec	2 tablespoons	30 milliliters
unsalted butter, cut into ½-inch pieces	¾ cup (1½ sticks)	170 grams
granulated sugar	1 cup	212 grams
large eggs	4	4
finely grated orange zest (from 1 orange)	2 teaspoons	4 grams
pure vanilla extract	1 teaspoon	5 milliliters

FOR THE SPICED MANDARINS

large mandarin oranges	5	454 grams
finely grated orange zest, preferably Valencia (from 2 oranges)	4 teaspoons	8 grams
freshly squeezed orange juice, preferably Valencia (from 2 oranges)	½ cup	125 milliliters
orange liqueur, such as Triple Sec	2 tablespoons	30 milliliters
whole cloves	2	2
star anise pod	1	1
vanilla bean, split lengthwise and seeds scraped out	1	1

(continued)

FRUIT CAKE

1. Preheat the oven to 350°F (180°C) with a rack in the center position. Brush a standard 8½ x 4½-inch loaf pan with Pan Goo.

2. In a small bowl, whisk together the flour, baking powder, salt, and 2 tablespoons (22 grams) of polenta. Set aside.

3. In a small saucepan, bring 1 cup (250 milliliters) of water and the orange liqueur to a boil over medium heat. Sprinkle in the remaining ¼ cup (44 grams) polenta while stirring constantly with a wooden spoon, letting the polenta fall at such a rate that you can see the individual granules as they tumble through the air. Return the mixture to a boil and continue cooking, stirring constantly, until you can see the bottom of the pan in the wake of the spoon, about 2 minutes. Remove the pan from the heat.

4. Whisk in the butter a few pieces at a time, until all of it has melted. The mixture will be very greasy. Whisk in the sugar, which will cool down the mixture so the eggs don't scramble. Whisk in the eggs one at a time, followed by the zest and vanilla. Stir in the flour mixture with the wooden spoon, then transfer the batter to the prepared pan. Tap the pan on the counter a few times to dislodge any large bubbles.

5. Bake until the cake is golden brown and springs back when gently pressed and a cake tester inserted in the center comes out clean, about 75 minutes, tenting with foil after an hour if the top is darkening too quickly.

6. Transfer the pan to a wire rack. Allow the cake to rest in the pan for 15 to 20 minutes, then carefully unmold it onto the rack to cool completely.

7. While the cake is in the oven, make the spiced mandarins: Peel the oranges and separate the segments, removing every last bit of pith you can stand to. Place in a medium bowl and add the orange zest and juice, orange liqueur, cloves, star anise, and vanilla seeds and pod. Let the flavors meld together for at least 1 hour. (The spiced mandarins can be made the day before and refrigerated.)

8. Serve slices of the pound cake with the mandarins and their juice.

STORAGE

The moisture from the polenta keeps this cake fresh, well wrapped, at room temperature for up to 1 week.

COCONUT APRICOT MACAROON CAKE

| MAKES 8 TO 10 SERVINGS | EASY |

This cake has the chew of a coconut macaroon and sweet-tart apricots strewn throughout. It's also one of those cakes that just seems to get better with age. Easy to make and hard to hold on to, it needs no accompaniment, but a little ice cream never hurt anything.

FOR THE CAKE

Pan Goo (page 224), for greasing the pan		
dried apricots, cut into ¼-inch pieces	1 cup	180 grams
apricot preserves	¼ cup	80 grams
unsweetened shredded coconut	½ cup	50 grams
all-purpose flour	1 cup	142 grams
baking powder	1 teaspoon	3 grams
coarse salt	1 teaspoon	3 grams
coconut oil, melted	6 tablespoons	84 grams
granulated sugar	1 cup	212 grams
large eggs	2	2
whole milk	⅓ cup	83 milliliters
pure vanilla extract	1 teaspoon	5 milliliters

FOR THE TOPPING

large egg white	1	1
granulated sugar	2 tablespoons	27 grams
coarse salt	1 pinch	1 pinch
unsweetened flaked coconut	1 cup	45 grams
sanding sugar, for sprinkling		

(continued)

1. Preheat the oven to 350°F (180°C) with a rack in the center position. Brush a 9 x 2-inch round cake pan with Pan Goo.

2. In a small saucepan, stir together the apricots, apricot preserves, and ¼ cup (62 milliliters) water. Set over medium heat and cook, stirring constantly with a wooden spoon, until a syrup forms that is thick enough to hold a line, about 5 minutes. Remove from the heat and toss with the shredded coconut. Set aside to cool slightly.

3. In a medium bowl, whisk together the flour, baking powder, and salt. Set aside.

4. In a large bowl, whisk the coconut oil, sugar, and eggs until smooth and creamy. Whisk in the milk and vanilla. Using a rubber spatula, stir the flour mixture into the wet ingredients. Gently fold the apricot situation into the batter, distributing it evenly throughout. Pour the batter into the prepared cake pan.

5. Make the topping: In a medium bowl, whisk the egg white, granulated sugar, and salt until just foamy, about 30 seconds. Stir in the coconut flakes and scatter on top of the cake batter. Sprinkle with sanding sugar.

6. Bake until the cake is firm to the touch and golden brown and a cake tester inserted into the center comes out with moist crumbs, about 1 hour.

7. Transfer the pan to a wire rack. Rest the cake in the pan for about 10 minutes, then unmold onto the rack to cool completely.

STORAGE

The cake will keep at room temperature, covered, for 3 or 4 days.

COCONUT POUND CAKE

| DAIRY-FREE | MAKES 8 TO 10 SERVINGS | EASY |

Here's to a cake that comes together entirely in a food processor, lickety-split! And since the delightful coconut flavor really shines after the cake has rested overnight, here's to planning ahead—and to patience, the most underrated of all the virtues.

Pan Goo (page 224), for greasing the pan		
unsweetened shredded coconut	1½ cups	150 grams
all-purpose flour	1½ cups	213 grams
granulated sugar	1¼ cups	265 grams
baking powder	2 teaspoons	6 grams
coarse salt	1 teaspoon	3 grams
freshly ground cardamom (see page 11)	1 teaspoon	2 grams
ground cinnamon	½ teaspoon	1.3 grams
coconut oil, melted	½ cup	112 grams
large eggs	4	4
unsweetened coconut milk	⅓ cup	83 milliliters
pure vanilla extract	2 teaspoons	10 milliliters
unsweetened flaked coconut	3 tablespoons	8 grams

1. Preheat the oven to 350°F (180°C) with a rack in the lower-third position. Brush a standard 8½ x 4½-inch loaf pan with Pan Goo.
2. In the bowl of a food processor, place the shredded coconut and flour and process for 1 to 2 minutes, until the coconut has been mostly ground into a fine powder. Add the sugar, baking powder, salt, cardamom, and cinnamon and pulse a few times to combine. With the food processor running, slowly pour the coconut oil through the feed tube, followed by the eggs, coconut milk, and vanilla. Process until smooth. Scrape the batter into the prepared pan and sprinkle with the coconut flakes.

3. Bake until the cake is firm to the touch and golden brown and a cake tester inserted into the center comes out with moist crumbs, about 75 minutes. Tent with foil for the last 15 minutes or so if the top is getting too dark.
4. Transfer the pan to a wire rack. Let the cake rest in the pan for about 15 minutes, then tip it out onto the rack to cool completely.

STORAGE
This cake tastes even better if you store it overnight in an airtight container at room temperature. It will keep well for 3 or 4 days.

OUT OF HAND

Knives and forks are overrated. These treats are finger-focused, perfect for pocketing or dressing to impress (if you're into that sort of thing).

But just because they're small doesn't mean they're to be overlooked. These diminutive delights are packed with flavors to enjoy from morning to night.

66	PINEAPPLE COCONUT BREAKFAST CAKES
69	JUMBO CRANBERRY PECAN MUFFINS
71	PUMPKIN CUPCAKES
74	ORANGE AND GOLDENBERRY PANFORTE
78	MANGO COCONUT CASHEW BITES
81	POPOVERS WITH PINEAPPLE JAM
82	RASPBERRY ALMOND PETIT FOURS
86	FIG AND DATE SNOWBALLS
88	ORANGE ZUCCHINI MUFFINS
90	BLUEBERRY GINGER STUDMUFFINS
92	STRAWBERRY TAMALES DE DULCE
96	ORANGE CURRANT ZALETI

PINEAPPLE COCONUT BREAKFAST CAKES

| MAKES 12 CAKES | EASY |

I knew from the outset that I wanted to temper the sweetness of pineapple with the nuttiness of spelt flour and coconut, making this recipe a little more breakfast appropriate. The small amount of honey helps to keep these cakes tender and moist even two days after baking.

spelt flour (but not whole spelt flour)	1½ cups	186 grams
unsweetened shredded coconut	¼ cup	25 grams
baking powder	1½ teaspoons	4.5 grams
coarse salt	½ teaspoon	1.5 grams
ground allspice	1 pinch	1 pinch
coconut oil, melted	⅓ cup	75 grams
firmly packed light brown sugar	½ cup	106 grams
honey	3 tablespoons	60 grams
large eggs	2	2
whole milk	⅓ cup	83 milliliters
pure vanilla extract	1 teaspoon	5 milliliters
roughly cut fresh pineapple, in ½-inch pieces	1 cup	160 grams

1. Preheat the oven to 425°F (220°C) with a rack in the center position. Line a standard 12-cup muffin pan with paper liners.

2. In a large bowl, whisk together the flour, coconut, baking powder, salt, and allspice. In another large bowl, whisk together the coconut oil, light brown sugar, honey, eggs, milk, and vanilla. Pour the wet ingredients over the dry and stir using a rubber spatula until everything is just about combined but a few lumps remain—it will look a lot like thick pancake batter. Stir in the pineapple and then divide the batter among the muffin wells, trying as hard as possible not to drip everywhere.

3. Bake the cakes for 5 minutes, then reduce the oven temperature to 375°F (190°C). Continue baking until the cakes are golden brown and just firm to the touch and a cake tester inserted into a center comes out clean, about 15 minutes.

4. Transfer the pan to a wire rack. Let the cakes rest in the pan for 5 minutes, then transfer them to the rack and let them cool completely before serving.

STORAGE

The cakes will keep well at room temperature in an airtight container for a day or even two.

JUMBO CRANBERRY PECAN MUFFINS

If you have friends or family visiting for the holidays, you could surprise them with these for breakfast one morning. You could also make them any other time, and it would be a much better surprise.

I think cranberries (the fresh or frozen kind, not the dried ones that pop up in salad bars when you have your back turned) are a completely underutilized berry. Where else can you get so much flavor in such a compact shape?

Pan Goo (page 224), optional		
old-fashioned oats	1 cup	92 grams
coarsely crumbled pecans, lightly toasted (see page 18), divided	1 cup	110 grams
all-purpose flour	1¼ cups	178 grams
ground cinnamon	2 teaspoons	5 grams
baking powder	1¾ teaspoons	5.3 grams
coarse salt	1¼ teaspoons	3.8 grams
baking soda	¼ teaspoon	1.5 grams
granulated sugar	⅔ cup	141 grams
pure maple syrup, preferably dark and robust	⅓ cup	112 grams
neutral oil, such as safflower	⅓ cup	83 milliliters
pure vanilla extract	1 tablespoon	15 milliliters
large eggs	2	2
sour cream	¾ cup	183 grams
finely grated orange zest (from 1 orange)	2 teaspoons	4 grams
fresh cranberries (thawed, if frozen)	2 cups	224 grams
sanding sugar, for sprinkling		

(continued)

1. Preheat the oven to 425°F (220°C). Line a 6-well jumbo muffin pan with paper liners or brush with Pan Goo.

2. In the bowl of a food processor, place the oats and ¼ cup (28 grams) of the pecans and pulse a few times until the mixture forms coarse crumbs, then process into a fine flour. Add the flour, cinnamon, baking powder, salt, and baking soda. Pulse a few times to combine, then transfer to a large bowl and set aside.

3. In another large bowl, whisk together the granulated sugar, maple syrup, oil, and vanilla until well combined. Whisk in the eggs, one at a time, followed by the sour cream and orange zest. Whisk vigorously until smooth.

4. Pulse the cranberries in the food processor about 16 times, until they are finely chopped but not pureed.

5. Make a well in the center of the flour mixture and add the wet ingredients. Working outward from the center of the bowl, stir the dry ingredients into the wet until no dry patches remain. It's okay if the mixture is still a little lumpy; it should look like a thick pancake batter. Gently fold the cranberries and remaining pecans into the batter. Divide evenly into the muffin wells, filling each to the top. Sprinkle with sanding sugar.

6. Bake the muffins for 5 minutes, then reduce the oven temperature to 375°F (190°C). Continue baking until the muffins spring back to the touch and a cake tester inserted into a center comes out with moist crumbs, about 30 minutes.

7. Transfer the pan to a wire rack. Let the muffins rest in the pan for about 5 minutes, then transfer them to the rack to cool completely.

STORAGE

Store the muffins in an airtight container at room temperature for a day or two.

PUMPKIN CUPCAKES

I can't get behind, nor will I deign to acronymize, pumpkin-spice this and that. There are places pumpkin simply should not be. I'll make an exception for these cupcakes.

Were it not for the frosting, these would be muffins, and they have the subtle sweetness and texture to prove it. But I've never turned down cream cheese frosting, and I don't suppose you would, either.

FOR THE CUPCAKES

Pan Goo (page 224), optional		
all-purpose flour	3 cups	426 grams
baking powder	1¾ teaspoons	5.3 grams
coarse salt	1½ teaspoons	4.5 grams
baking soda	½ teaspoon	3 grams
pure pumpkin puree (not pumpkin pie filling)	1 can (15 ounces)	425 grams
ground cinnamon	1 tablespoon	7.5 grams
ground allspice	¾ teaspoon	1.5 grams
freshly grated nutmeg (see page 12)	10 seconds (about ½ teaspoon)	1 gram
ancho chile powder (see page 73)	½ teaspoon	1.5 grams
neutral oil, such as safflower	½ cup	125 milliliters
firmly packed dark brown sugar	2 cups	424 grams
sour cream	½ cup	122 grams
large eggs	3 whole, plus 1 yolk	3 whole, plus 1 yolk
pure vanilla extract	1 tablespoon	15 milliliters
roasted salted pepitas, finely chopped, plus additional for garnish	½ cup	75 grams

FOR FINISHING

Tangy Cream Cheese Frosting (page 230)	1 recipe	1 recipe

(continued)

1. Preheat the oven to 425°F (220°C) with a rack in the center position. Line two standard 12-cup muffin pans with paper liners or brush with Pan Goo.

2. In a large bowl, whisk together the flour, baking powder, salt, and baking soda and set aside.

3. In a small saucepan, combine the pumpkin puree and spices and set over medium-high heat. Cook, stirring frequently with a wooden spoon, until the mixture bubbles and steams like a tar pit, about 8 minutes. Remove the pan from the heat and whisk in the oil and dark brown sugar. Set aside to cool slightly, then whisk in the sour cream, eggs, yolk, and vanilla.

4. Make a well in the center of the flour mixture and add the wet ingredients. Starting in the center of the bowl, stir the dry ingredients into the wet with a rubber spatula until the mixture forms a thick, slightly lumpy batter. Be careful not to overwork it. Gently stir in the chopped pepitas. Divide the batter among the prepared muffin wells, filling each with about ¼ cup of batter.

5. Bake the cupcakes for 5 minutes, then reduce the oven temperature to 375°F (190°C) and continue baking until the cakes are firm and spring back to the touch and a cake tester inserted into a center comes out with moist crumbs, 10 to 12 minutes.

6. Transfer the pan to a rack. Allow the cupcakes to rest in the pan for 5 minutes, then unmold them onto the rack and let them cool completely. Dollop each with Tangy Cream Cheese Frosting and a sprinkling of pepitas.

STORAGE

Store the cakes, loosely covered, in a cool spot or refrigerate for up to 1 day. Serve at room temperature.

ANCHO CHILE POWDER

Ancho chiles, which are dried poblano peppers, are gently warming but not spicy. Add a pinch of cayenne pepper to the batter if you want these cupcakes to burn.

ORANGE AND GOLDENBERRY PANFORTE

| DAIRY-FREE | MAKES ABOUT 20 SERVINGS | INTERMEDIATE | SPECIAL EQUIPMENT: 9-INCH SPRINGFORM PAN, PASTRY BRUSH, CANDY THERMOMETER |

This traditional Italian confection walks the line between candy and cake, with a texture similar to nougat (but with much less fuss).

Pan Goo (page 224), for greasing the pan		
raw hazelnuts	1 cup	128 grams
all-purpose flour	1 cup	142 grams
unsweetened cocoa powder, preferably Dutch-processed	2 tablespoons	10 grams
ground cinnamon	1 teaspoon	2.5 grams
ground ginger	1 teaspoon	2.8 grams
coarse salt	1 teaspoon	3 grams
ground cayenne pepper, or to taste	¼ teaspoon	0.5 gram
ground mace (see page 77)	1 pinch	1 pinch
whole unsalted roasted almonds, coarsely chopped	1 cup	162 grams
finely diced candied orange peel (page 236)	1 cup	180 grams
dried goldenberries, coarsely chopped	½ cup	75 grams
cocoa nibs	2 tablespoons	15 grams
best-quality semisweet chocolate, preferably about 65% cacao, melted and cooled	3 ounces	85 grams
granulated sugar	1 cup	212 grams
honey	½ cup plus 2 tablespoons	200 grams
confectioners' sugar, for dusting		

(continued)

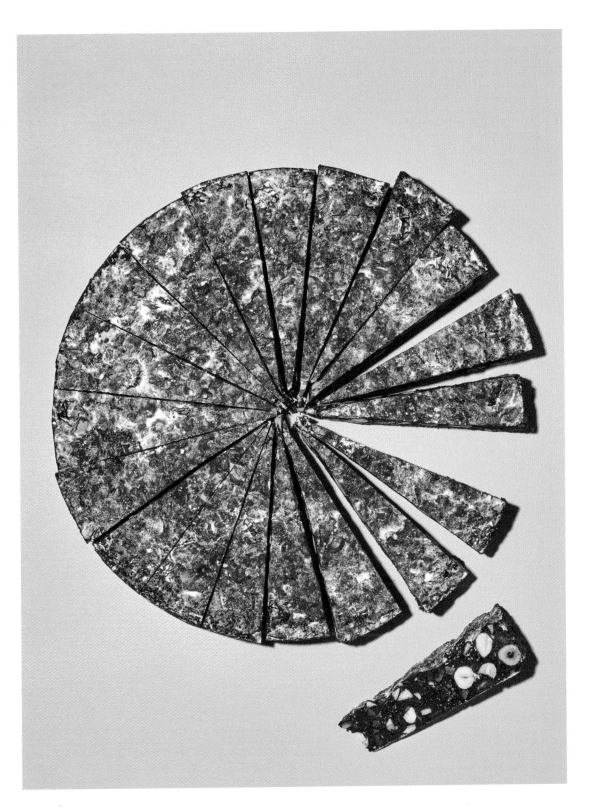

1. Preheat the oven to 300°F (150°C) with a rack in the center position. Brush a 9-inch springform pan with Pan Goo and line the bottom with parchment paper.

2. Place the hazelnuts on a rimmed baking sheet and roast until the skins blister and the nuts begin to turn golden brown, about 14 minutes. Place the hot nuts in the center of a clean, lint-free kitchen towel and gather the edges like a beggar's purse. Set aside until cool enough to handle, then rub the nuts with the kitchen towel to dislodge the skins. (Alternatively, buy blanched hazelnuts and save yourself the trouble.)

3. In a large heatproof bowl, whisk together the flour, cocoa powder, cinnamon, ginger, salt, cayenne pepper, and a generous pinch of mace. Stir the hazelnuts, almonds, candied orange peel, goldenberries, and cocoa nibs into the flour mixture, tossing them through your fingers to break up the clumps. Stir the melted chocolate into the mixture as best you can, but don't worry about getting it perfectly distributed.

4. In a small saucepan, stir the granulated sugar and honey together with a rubber spatula until all the sugar has been moistened. Brush down the sides of the pot with a wet pastry brush to remove any sugar crystals clinging to the edges.

Place a candy thermometer in the pan and set over high heat, tilting the pan slightly to fully submerge the bottom of the thermometer if necessary. Cook without stirring until the syrup reaches 240°F (116°C), 3 to 5 minutes.

5. Immediately, but carefully, pour the hot syrup into the flour mixture and stir with a heatproof rubber spatula until a sticky dough forms. Scrape into the prepared springform pan and press to the edges using the back of a spoon that's been dipped in water. Bake the cake until the surface is matte and the outer edges begin to blister, about 45 minutes.

6. Dust with confectioners' sugar just as the cake comes out of the oven. Allow the cake to cool completely in the pan, then run a knife around the outside edge and remove the collar. Flip the cake onto a cutting board and peel off the parchment paper, then reinvert and use a sharp knife to cut slender servings. Dust again with a fresh coat of confectioners' sugar, if desired.

STORAGE

Panforte will keep at room temperature in an airtight container more or less forever.

MACE

Mace and nutmeg are kindred spices, both derived from the edible yellow fruit of *Myristica fragrans*, an evergreen tree native to Indonesia. Mace is the lacy coating, or aril, that surrounds the seed. The kernel of that seed is the more familiar nutmeg.

MANGO COCONUT CASHEW BITES

| DAIRY-FREE | MAKES 24 TWO-BITE CAKES | EASY |
| SPECIAL EQUIPMENT: MINI-MUFFIN PAN |

These two-bite treats are subtly sweet, with an earthy undertone that comes from the turmeric and ginger. Perfect in the late afternoon. Even better the next morning.

coconut oil, melted, plus additional for brushing	6 tablespoons	84 grams
unsalted roasted cashews	½ cup	64 grams
freeze-dried mango	⅓ cup (½ ounce)	14 grams
cake flour	⅓ cup	38 grams
unsweetened shredded coconut	⅓ cup	33 grams
ground turmeric	¼ teaspoon	0.5 gram
ground ginger	1 teaspoon	2.8 grams
granulated sugar, divided	⅓ cup plus 2 tablespoons	71 grams plus 27 grams
large egg whites	3	3
thinly sliced fresh mango, in ½-inch pieces	⅓ cup	55 grams

1. Preheat the oven to 325°F (170°C) with a rack in the upper-third position. Generously brush a 24-cup mini-muffin pan with coconut oil.

2. Pulse the cashews and freeze-dried mango in a food processor until finely ground but not a paste, about 30 seconds. The mango pieces may stay a bit coarse. Don't worry about it.

3. Transfer the cashew and mango mixture to a medium bowl and whisk in the flour, coconut, turmeric, ginger, and ⅓ cup (71 grams) of the sugar, then stir in the coconut oil with a rubber spatula until a crumbly mixture forms.

4. In another medium bowl, whisk the egg whites and remaining 2 tablespoons (27 grams) of sugar until they're the consistency of the foam on a poorly made cappuccino. Whisk the egg whites into the crumbly mixture. Divide the batter into the prepared mini-muffin pan, filling each cup about halfway (with about 1 tablespoon of batter). Scatter the fresh mango pieces on top, placing one or two per cup, depending on their size.

5. Bake until the cakes are just golden around the edges and the tops are no longer sticky, about 15 minutes.

6. Transfer the pan to a wire rack. Use a small offset spatula to transfer the warm cakes to the rack to cool completely.

STORAGE

The cakes will keep for 3 to 4 days in an airtight container at room temperature.

POPOVERS WITH PINEAPPLE JAM

| MAKES 6 SERVINGS | INTERMEDIATE |
| SPECIAL EQUIPMENT: CANDY THERMOMETER, POPOVER PAN |

I've found the secret to perfect popovers is in the temperature of the batter and working quickly to get the pan back into the oven lickety-split. That's why I've broken my own rules and used nonstick cooking spray to grease the pan. It's the safest, fastest way to go.

large eggs, truly, madly, deeply room temperature	3	3
whole milk	1½ cups	375 milliliters
unsalted butter	4 tablespoons (½ stick)	57 grams
coarse salt	1 teaspoon	3 grams
all-purpose flour	1⅓ cups	189 grams
nonstick cooking spray, preferably organic		
Pineapple Jam (page 241), for serving		

1. Preheat the oven to 450°F (230°C) and place a rack on the lowest level (and remove the other racks). Place a standard 6-well popover pan on the rack.

2. Warm the eggs in a bowl of hot water for about 10 minutes.

3. In a small saucepan, heat the milk, butter, and salt until the temperature reaches 130°F (54°C) on a candy thermometer. Transfer the mixture to a large bowl and whisk in the eggs until foamy. Add the flour in three additions and whisk until the batter is almost completely smooth. It's okay to leave a few small lumps. The batter will have cooled to about 95°F (35°C).

4. Carefully remove the popover pan from the oven and quickly coat with nonstick cooking spray. Divide the batter among the wells, filling each one most of the way to the top. Cautiously, but expeditiously, return the pan to the oven and set a timer for 20 minutes. If, like me, your idea of baking involves sitting in front of the oven, nose pressed to the glass, I'll say this: Turn off the light and walk away. Popovers take their shape slowly.*

5. After 20 minutes, reduce the oven temperature to 350°F (180°C) and continue baking without opening the door for 35 minutes, or until the popovers are deep golden brown and crisp.

6. Slip the popovers out of the pan and onto a wire rack as soon as they come out of the oven. Use a paring knife to cut a small vent somewhere inconspicuous on each to let out some of the steam.

7. Serve immediately with Pineapple Jam.

---

* I know you're going to watch, so you might as well be prepared. Here's what is going to happen: The batter will begin to rise from the outside in. At 10 minutes you may see a sinkhole in the center. After 20 minutes they will have puffed significantly but still be far from explosive. They will continue to puff during the final 35 minutes of baking at the reduced temperature and take on their characteristic whimsical shapes. I promise.

RASPBERRY ALMOND PETIT FOURS

| MAKES ABOUT 2 DOZEN | INTERMEDIATE |
| SPECIAL EQUIPMENT: TWO 9 X 13-INCH RIMMED BAKING SHEETS | OVERNIGHT |

It wouldn't be teatime without two-bite treats like these. Once you've tasted them, you might find it wouldn't be 9 a.m. (or midnight) either. Though small in stature, these cakes are packed with flavor. Use the best jam you can find (homemade, if you've got it).

FOR THE CAKE LAYERS

Pan Goo (page 224), for greasing the pan		
all-purpose flour	1 cup	142 grams
coarse salt	1 teaspoon	3 grams
baking powder	½ teaspoon	1.5 grams
almond paste (not marzipan)	7 ounces (about ½ cup)	198 grams
unsalted butter, softened	½ cup (1 stick)	113 grams
granulated sugar, divided	½ cup	106 grams
large eggs, separated	4	4
whole milk	¼ cup	62 milliliters
pure vanilla extract	1 tablespoon	15 milliliters

FOR ASSEMBLY AND FINISHING

raspberry jam or Any Berry Jam (page 239)	⅔ cup	213 grams
best-quality dark chocolate, preferably around 65% cacao, finely chopped	4 ounces	113 grams
freeze-dried raspberries	1 tablespoon	2 grams

1. Preheat the oven to 350°F (180°C) with a rack in the center position. Line a 13 x 18-inch rimmed baking sheet with a silicone baking mat or parchment paper and brush with Pan Goo.

2. In a small bowl, whisk together the flour, salt, and baking powder. Set aside.

3. In the bowl of a food processor, place the almond paste, butter, and ¼ cup (53 grams) of the sugar and process 1 to 2 minutes, until very smooth, stopping to scrape the sides of the bowl occasionally. With the machine running, add the yolks through the feed tube one at a time, followed by the milk and vanilla, then process about 30 seconds longer. Scrape the bowl again and add the dry ingredients. Pulse 8 to 10 times, until just combined. Scrape the batter into a large bowl and set aside.

(continued)

FRUIT CAKE

4. In the bowl of an electric mixer fitted with the whisk attachment, begin whipping the egg whites on medium speed until frothy, then slowly shake in the remaining ¼ cup (53 grams) of sugar while gradually increasing the mixer speed to high. Continue whipping until the egg whites form stiff peaks.

5. Lighten the batter by whisking in about one third of the egg whites, then gently fold in the remaining egg whites in two additions. Pour the batter into the prepared baking sheet and smooth the top with an offset spatula.

6. Bake the cake until the center springs back to the touch and a cake tester inserted into the center comes out clean, 18 to 20 minutes. Remove the baking sheet from the oven and allow the cake to cool completely on the baking sheet.

7. Invert the cake onto a cutting board and remove the baking mat or parchment paper. Using a sharp serrated knife, cut the cake crosswise into thirds. Place one section of cake on a parchment- or wax-paper-lined 9 x 13-inch rimmed baking sheet and spread ⅓ cup (106 grams) of the jam over the top, leaving about a ½-inch border. Layer with a second piece of cake and spread with the remaining ⅓ cup (106 grams) of jam. Layer the third piece of cake on top and cover with a piece of parchment or wax paper.

8. Place a second 9 x 13-inch rimmed baking sheet on top of the cake and weigh it down with some heavy pantry items; canned goods work well. Refrigerate the whole shebang for at least 4 hours or overnight.

9. Place about half the chocolate in a heatproof bowl set over a pan of gently simmering water. Stir constantly with a rubber spatula until just melted, about 2 minutes. Remove from the heat and add the remaining chocolate. Stir vigorously until completely melted. Use an offset spatula to spread an even layer over the top of the cake. Refrigerate until the chocolate has just set, 5 to 10 minutes.

10. Transfer the cake to a cutting board. Heat the blade of a sharp knife with a kitchen torch or by dipping in a bowl of just-boiled water and drying with a kitchen towel. Use the knife to trim the edges into a tidy rectangle, then cut the cake into bars, each about 1 x 2 inches, reheating the knife as needed to cut clean slices.

11. Just before serving, press the freeze-dried raspberries through a fine-mesh sieve to create a powder, dusting the cakes here and there. Serve chilled or at cool room temperature.

STORAGE

The petit fours can be stored in an airtight container in the refrigerator for up to 1 week.

WORKING WITH CHOCOLATE

Savvy bakers may prefer to properly temper the chocolate instead of simply melting half as I've done here. This would allow the cakes to sit at room temperature for longer without your having to worry about the chocolate melting. Do so if you wish, but I think it's unnecessary. Storing the cakes in the refrigerator obviates that concern, and they are delicious chilled.

The oven's preheated

The butter's well-beated

The dry's folded into the wet

The chocolate is melted

The vanilla sweet smellded

The timer is precisely set

The pan has been filled

Anticipation builds

Will it be a delight or a dread?

I forgot the sugar

Too late to recover

F#©k it I'm going to bed

FIG AND DATE SNOWBALLS

| GLUTEN-FREE, DAIRY-FREE | MAKES ABOUT 28 | EASY |

We all have mountains to climb. Whether yours are snow packed or of the laundry persuasion, these treats will give you the strength you need to persevere.

dried figs, stemmed and halved	2 cups	380 grams
tawny port	½ cup	125 milliliters
Medjool dates, pitted	2 cups	386 grams
unsweetened shredded coconut, divided	1 cup	100 grams
cocoa nibs, optional	2 tablespoons	15 grams
coarse salt	1 pinch	1 pinch
almonds, lightly toasted (see page 18)	28 (about ¼ cup)	40 grams

1. In a small saucepan, cook the figs and port over medium heat, stirring frequently with a wooden spoon, until the seeds release from the figs and the port thickens, about 5 minutes.

2. Transfer the cooked figs and what's left of the port to a food processor along with the dates, ¼ cup (25 grams) of coconut, the cocoa nibs, if using, and salt. Process until the mixture forms a stiff, sticky, satisfying paste, about 1 minute.

3. Shape heaping tablespoons of the mixture into rough balls and press an almond into the center of each. Roll the balls between the heels of your hands to round them out, then toss in the remaining ¾ cup (75 grams) coconut to coat.

STORAGE

Store in an airtight container at cool room temperature for a month, or in the refrigerator basically forever.

ORANGE ZUCCHINI MUFFINS

| MAKES 12 MUFFINS | INTERMEDIATE |
| SPECIAL EQUIPMENT: NUT MILK BAG OR CHEESECLOTH |

Like all squash, zucchini are fruit, more closely related to melons than your typical garden greens.

Who cares? These are an orange lover's muffin. But despair not for zucchini; misunderstood but not forgotten, it provides just enough body to give this batter its characteristic bite.

Pan Goo (page 224), optional		
coarsely grated zucchini, gently packed (from 1 large zucchini)	1½ cups	240 grams
all-purpose flour	1½ cups	213 grams
ground cinnamon	1 teaspoon	2.5 grams
baking powder	1 teaspoon	3 grams
coarse salt	½ teaspoon	1.5 grams
baking soda	¼ teaspoon	1.5 grams
granulated sugar	½ cup	106 grams
firmly packed light brown sugar	¼ cup	53 grams
orange marmalade	⅓ cup	80 grams
unsalted butter, melted and cooled	½ cup (1 stick)	113 grams
large eggs	2	2
pure vanilla extract	1½ teaspoons	7.5 milliliters
navel orange	1	131 grams
orange liqueur, such as Triple Sec	2 tablespoons	30 milliliters
turbinado sugar, for sprinkling		

1. Preheat the oven to 425°F (220°C) with a rack in the center position. Line a standard 12-cup muffin pan with paper liners or brush the wells with Pan Goo.

2. Over a bowl or sink, firmly squeeze the zucchini in a nut milk bag or a double layer of cheesecloth until no more liquid comes out, then fluff the zucchini and squeeze it again; you'll be surprised by how much liquid was left. Try to get the zucchini as dry as possible.

3. In a small bowl, whisk together the flour, cinnamon, baking powder, salt, and baking soda. Set aside.

4. In a large bowl, whisk the granulated sugar and light brown sugar with the marmalade and butter. Whisk in the eggs, one at a time, and then

add the vanilla. Zest the orange into the sugar mixture with a rasp grater, then supreme the segments (see page 248) and set aside. Squeeze every last drop of juice from the leftover orange membrane into the sugar situation. Add the orange liqueur and whisk well. Stir in the zucchini with a rubber spatula and then gently stir in the dry ingredients until just combined.

5. Divide the batter evenly into the muffin wells, filling each one about three quarters of the way up. Chop the orange supremes into 1-inch pieces and arrange them on top of the batter, then sprinkle everything with turbinado sugar.

6. Bake the muffins for 5 minutes, then reduce the temperature to 375°F (190°C). Continue baking until the muffins are golden brown and firm to the touch and a cake tester inserted into a center comes out with moist crumbs, 18 to 20 minutes.

7. Transfer the pan to a wire rack. Let the muffins rest in the pan for about 5 minutes, then transfer them to the rack to cool completely.

STORAGE

These muffins are best the day you bake them, but they will keep for a day or two at room temperature, loosely covered.

BLUEBERRY GINGER STUDMUFFINS

| MAKES 12 MUFFINS | EASY |

Get it? Because they're studded with blueberries. And they're hot.

all-purpose flour, divided	2¼ cups plus 1 tablespoon	320 grams plus 9 grams
baking powder	1¾ teaspoons	5.3 grams
coarse salt	1¼ teaspoons	3.8 grams
baking soda	¼ teaspoon	1.5 grams
fresh blueberries (thawed, if frozen)	2 cups	280 grams
neutral oil, such as safflower	⅓ cup	83 milliliters
large eggs	2	2
granulated sugar, plus additional for sprinkling	1 cup	212 grams
plain whole-milk Greek yogurt	1 cup	250 grams
finely grated lemon zest (from 1 lemon)	1 teaspoon	2 grams
freshly squeezed lemon juice (from 1 lemon)	2 tablespoons	30 milliliters
freshly grated ginger, lightly packed	2 tablespoons	30 grams
very finely chopped candied ginger	¼ cup	41 grams

1. Preheat the oven to 425°F (220°C) with a rack in the center position. Line a standard 12-cup muffin pan with paper liners.

2. In a large bowl, whisk 2¼ cups (320 grams) of the flour with the baking powder, salt, and baking soda and set aside. In a small bowl, toss the blueberries with the remaining 1 tablespoon (9 grams) of flour.

3. In another large bowl, combine the oil, eggs, sugar, yogurt, and lemon zest and juice and set aside.

4. Over a small bowl, squeeze the ginger through a sturdy paper towel or double layer of cheesecloth, extracting as much of the juice as possible, until you have about 2 tablespoons (30 milliliters). Discard the pulp. Whisk the juice into the sugar mixture to combine.

5. Make a well in the center of the flour mixture and add the wet ingredients. Using a rubber spatula, stir the dry ingredients into the wet, working outward from the center of the bowl. When all of the flour has been moistened but some lumps remain, gently fold in the blueberries and candied ginger. Divide the mixture into the muffin pan, filling each well to the brim. Sprinkle the tops of the muffins gratuitously with sugar.

6. Bake the muffins for 5 minutes, then reduce the oven temperature to 375°F (190°C). Continue baking until the muffins are golden on the edges and firm to the touch and a cake tester

inserted into a center comes out with moist crumbs, about 20 minutes.

7. Transfer the pan to a wire rack. Let the muffins rest in the pan for about 5 minutes, then transfer them to the rack to cool completely.

STORAGE
Store at room temperature in an airtight container for up to 2 days.

STRAWBERRY TAMALES DE DULCE

| GLUTEN-FREE | MAKES ABOUT 16 TAMALES | EASY |

"Para todo mal, un tamal. Para todo bien, también."

Eddie's taught me that tamales are the perfect party food because it's really no harder to make eight batches than it is to make one, provided you have enough friends to help. They're also infinitely adjustable; you can fill them with just about anything you can dream up. His sister's famous strawberry tamales inspired this recipe.

When you crack open the lid of your tamale pot and that first burst of steam puffs out, it's hard not to imagine the sunlight dappling through the jacaranda trees on Avenida Amsterdam. You could be transported just by the sight of it. Unless you're already there, in which case—jealous!

hojas para tamales (dried corn husks)	18	18
masa harina (prepared corn flour), such as Maseca	2¼ cups	290 grams
baking powder	2 teaspoons	6 grams
coarse salt	½ teaspoon	1.5 grams
granulated sugar	½ cup	106 grams
ground ginger	½ teaspoon	1.4 grams
unsalted butter, softened	½ cup (1 stick)	113 grams
whole milk	1 cup	250 milliliters
strawberry jam, Any Berry Jam (page 239), or at least a really good jam	about ¾ cup	about 240 grams
heavy cream	1 cup	250 milliliters
confectioners' sugar	2 tablespoons	14 grams

1. Start off by soaking the hojas in a very large bowl of cool water. You'll need about 16 for the tamales, and a few extra to tear into the strips you'll use to tie them shut. Bathe the hojas in the water until they're soft enough to bend without cracking, then drain and shake off as much water as possible. Set aside while you mix the masa.

2. In a large bowl, whisk together the masa harina, baking powder, salt, sugar, and ground ginger. Use your fingers to rub the butter into the flour mixture until it's more or less the texture of brown sugar—not exactly clumpy, but not dry, either. Then make a well in the center of the bowl and pour in the milk. Use a wooden spoon to stir the dry ingredients into the milk, working

(continued)

out from the center, until all of it has been moistened. You'll end up with something along the lines of a thick biscuit dough. Let the dough rest for 10 minutes or so.

3. Clean off your counter—assembling tamales takes up more space than you think it will. Now's a good time for your friends to arrive, because tamales are party food, and this party is interactive.

4. Scoop about 3 tablespoons (44 grams) of dough onto the lower half of an hoja and use your fingers to spread it into a rectangle that's about 3 x 4 inches, or however big the husk will allow, keeping about ½ inch away from the edges. Spread a scant 1 tablespoon of jam in a line down the center of the dough. Pick up the tamal with both hands and use the husk to pinch the dough closed around the jam, sealing it as tightly as possible,* then close the husk around the tamal, cardigan style. Fold the (empty) top half of the hoja down to meet the bottom and use a thin ribbon torn from an extra hoja to tie the tamal closed in a perfect little package.

* Which is to say, not all that tight.

5. Place a steamer basket in what I'm guessing is your largest pot with a tight-fitting lid and add enough water to come just below the basket. Bring the water to a boil over high heat, then carefully place the tamales in the basket, standing them up on their folded ends. Cover the pot and steam on high heat until they're firm and release easily from the hojas, about 50 minutes. Check the water level in the pot periodically and add more hot water as needed.

6. Let the tamales cool for just a few minutes before serving, but they absolutely cannot be served cold. While you wait, whip the heavy cream with the confectioners' sugar until soft peaks form. Serve the warm tamales with the whipped cream passed on the side.

STORAGE

You can store the tamales in an airtight container in the refrigerator overnight and reheat, still wrapped in their husks, in the steamer basket over gently simmering water, but they're best served right away.

PLANNING AHEAD

The tamales can be assembled through step 4 the day before serving. Store them in an airtight container in the refrigerator and steam them just before serving.

ORANGE CURRANT ZALETI

These not-so-sweet Italian treats are crumbly and flaky and disappear with alacrity. Be careful: Overbake them and miss out on their soft, tender interiors. Some might call them a cookie. Don't.

FOR THE DOUGH

dried currants	¾ cup	104 grams
finely grated orange zest (from 1 orange)	2 teaspoons	4 grams
freshly squeezed orange juice (from 1 orange)	2 tablespoons	30 milliliters
pure vanilla extract	1 teaspoon	5 milliliters
almond extract	1 teaspoon	5 milliliters
quick-cooking (but not instant) polenta	1¼ cups	220 grams
all-purpose flour	1¼ cups	178 grams
baking powder	1½ teaspoons	4.5 grams
granulated sugar	¼ cup	53 grams
coarse salt	½ teaspoon	1.5 grams
unsalted cultured butter, cold and cut into ½-inch pieces	¾ cup (1½ sticks)	170 grams
large eggs, lightly beaten	1 whole, plus 1 yolk	1 whole, plus 1 yolk

FOR FINISHING

large egg white, lightly beaten	1	1
sanding sugar, for sprinkling		

1. In a small bowl, stir together the currants, orange zest and juice, vanilla, and almond extract. Set aside for about 20 minutes so the currants can absorb some of the liquid.

2. In a large bowl, whisk together the polenta, flour, baking powder, granulated sugar, and salt. With nimble fingers, rub the butter into the polenta mixture until it's sandy and holds together when squeezed gently. Add the lightly beaten egg and yolk, the currants, and any of the liquid that remains. Stir with a wooden spoon until there are no dry patches.

3. Scrape the dough onto a piece of parchment or wax paper and form into a 7-inch square that's about 1 inch thick. Wrap well and refrigerate until the dough is very firm, at least 1 hour and up to 2 days.

4. Preheat the oven to 350°F (180°C) with a rack in the center position. Line a 13 x 18-inch rimmed baking sheet with a silicone baking mat or parchment paper. Using a sharp knife, cut the dough into 1-inch-wide strips and then cut crosswise into 1-inch squares.

5. Arrange the squares on the prepared baking sheet, leaving about 1 inch of space between each. Brush the tops with the egg white and sprinkle with sanding sugar.

6. Bake until the edges are lightly golden, 15 to 18 minutes, then transfer to a wire rack to cool.

STORAGE

These keep well in an airtight container for a few days or more.

SHOWSTOPPERS

I'm not the kind of guy who runs into the spotlight; I'd rather do the hard work behind the scenes and let the results speak for themselves. These cakes do just that. I don't want to say that they're difficult, so I'm going to call them *rewarding*.

One thing you'll notice straightaway about these recipes is that they're largely comprised of multiple components. The challenge is not strictly in technique; it's in the timing. But with a little planning, even the most complicated projects can be broken down into manageable pieces.

The really crucial thing is that no matter how many questions your friends and family ask, your answer is always the same: "Oh, it was no big deal. I just threw it together."

100	PEANUT BUTTER AND JELLY CAKE
103	CHOCOLATE CARAMEL BANANA ROULADE
107	MAMEY CHEESECAKE
111	STRAWBERRY FOOLS
112	KEY LIME CAKE
115	HUMMINGBIRD LAYER CAKE
118	PASSION FRUIT LIME PAVLOVA
122	SUMMER BERRY SHORTCAKES
125	CRANBERRY YULE LOG
129	COCONUT CIELO CAKE
132	RASPBERRY DACQUOISE CAKE
135	HORCHATA AND ROASTED PLUM SORBET CAKE
139	UME-SHISO WATERMELON FROZEN YOGURT CAKE
141	GUAVA CREPE CAKE
146	KIWI AND GOLDENBERRY SARATOGA TORTE

PEANUT BUTTER AND JELLY CAKE

| MAKES 12 SERVINGS | EASY |

I *love* peanut butter. It's what I would take to a desert island, on a road trip, and possibly to my grave. I prefer natural peanut butter—the kind with only two ingredients that needs to be lovingly stirred back together—for my spoon licking and toast spreading, but I've learned (reluctantly) that it's a poor choice when it comes to baking. It weighs down and toughens batters; trust me, that's not what you're after. Go with something unnatural here.

This cake bakes up with a creamy texture and irresistibly peanutty flavor, just savory enough to balance the sweetness of the jam and berries. It's a cake that you might have to hide from your children—or yourself.

Pan Goo (page 224), for greasing the pan		
all-purpose flour	¾ cup	107 grams
baking powder	¾ teaspoon	2.3 grams
coarse salt	½ teaspoon	1.5 grams
smooth peanut butter (not natural)	½ cup	128 grams
unsalted butter, softened	4 tablespoons (½ stick)	57 grams
firmly packed light brown sugar	¾ cup	159 grams
large eggs	1 whole, plus 1 yolk	1 whole, plus 1 yolk
whole milk	⅓ cup	83 milliliters
pure vanilla extract	1 teaspoon	5 milliliters
strawberry jam or Any Berry Jam (page 239)	⅓ cup	107 grams
strawberries, the largest ones cut into halves or quarters	1 pound	454 grams

1. Preheat the oven to 350°F (180°C) with a rack in the center position. Brush a 9 x 2-inch round cake pan with Pan Goo.

2. In a medium bowl, whisk together the flour, baking powder, and salt. Set aside.

3. In the bowl of an electric mixer fitted with the paddle attachment, combine the peanut butter, butter, and light brown sugar. Beat together on medium speed until the mixture is smooth and

very creamy, about 3 minutes. Stop the mixer, scrape down the sides of the bowl, and add the egg and yolk. Continue beating on medium speed until the egg has been completely incorporated into the batter, about 1 minute longer.

4. With the mixer running on low speed, add half the flour mixture, beating until just combined. Scrape down the sides of the bowl and continue mixing on low speed while slowly adding the milk

(continued)

and vanilla. Add the remaining flour mixture and stir by hand until smooth. Scrape the batter into the prepared pan and smooth the top with a small offset spatula.

5. Bake until the cake is just firm to the touch and a cake tester inserted into the center comes out with moist crumbs, about 25 minutes.

6. Transfer the pan to a wire rack. Allow the cake to rest in the pan for 10 minutes before inverting it onto the rack to cool completely.

7. Transfer the cake to a serving platter. Be careful, because the underside may want to stick to the cooling rack. (It's a sign of how delicious the cake will be.) Spread the jam over the top of the cake, leaving about a ½-inch border around the edges, and then pile high with strawberries. Try not to dig in before your guests arrive.

STORAGE

This cake stores well enough in the refrigerator, but you're not going to have to worry about that for long.

CHOCOLATE CARAMEL BANANA ROULADE

My friend Liz insists that bananas are a "bully" flavor. I love them, but I can agree. Their sweetness can overpower delicate situations, which is why I've kept them to themselves, paired with their best counterparts: chocolate, caramel, and rum.

FOR THE CARAMEL FILLING

granulated sugar	¾ cup	159 grams
heavy cream, warmed slightly	½ cup	125 milliliters
dark rum	2 tablespoons	30 milliliters
pure vanilla extract	1 tablespoon	15 milliliters
coarse salt	¾ teaspoon	2.3 grams
cream cheese, softened	½ cup (4 ounces)	113 grams
unsalted butter, softened	4 tablespoons (½ stick)	57 grams
confectioners' sugar	½ cup	57 grams

FOR THE CHOCOLATE ROULADE

Pan Goo (page 224), for greasing the pan		
cake flour	1¼ cups	141 grams
unsweetened cocoa powder, preferably Dutch-processed, plus additional for dusting	¼ cup	20 grams
coarse salt	½ teaspoon	1.5 grams
baking soda	¼ teaspoon	1.5 grams
large eggs, separated	6	6
granulated sugar, divided	1 cup	212 grams
buttermilk	½ cup	125 milliliters
neutral oil, such as safflower	¼ cup	62 milliliters
pure vanilla extract	1 teaspoon	5 milliliters
instant espresso powder	¼ teaspoon	0.5 gram

(continued) **103**

banana, sliced into coins about ¼ inch thick	1	120 grams
best-quality semisweet chocolate, preferably about 65% cacao, finely chopped	6 ounces	170 grams
heavy cream	½ cup	125 milliliters
flaky sea salt, for sprinkling		

1. Begin by making a caramel sauce: In a small, heavy saucepan, place the granulated sugar with ¼ cup (62 milliliters) water and bring to a boil over medium-high heat. Stir the sugar gently until it dissolves, but stop stirring when the syrup reaches a boil. Try to avoid splashing the sides of the pot; if you do, use a pastry brush moistened with water to brush away any crystals that form. Keep cooking the syrup, swirling the pan occasionally, until it turns light amber, about 5 minutes.

2. Turn off the heat and allow the syrup to continue cooking by carryover heat until it is quite dark. If you see just a wisp or two of smoke, you've hit the jackpot. Immediately begin adding the cream to the hot caramel in a slow, steady stream. Be careful—it will bubble up and steam vehemently. Return the pan to medium heat and insert a candy thermometer.

3. Cook until the syrup reaches thread stage (230°F, 110°C), tilting the pan as needed to get a good read. Pour what is now a sauce into a heatproof bowl and quickly stir in the rum, vanilla, and coarse salt. Set aside to cool to room temperature. You can store it, covered, in the refrigerator for up to 1 week. Just be sure to bring it back to room temperature before using.

4. In the bowl of an electric mixer fitted with the paddle attachment, combine the cream cheese, butter, confectioners' sugar, and the room-temperature caramel sauce. Beat on medium speed, stopping to scrape down the sides of the bowl occasionally, until the mixture is light and fluffy, about 3 minutes. Transfer to a small bowl and refrigerate for at least 2 hours or overnight, until you're ready to fill the cake, which I realize you probably aren't because I haven't told you how to make it yet.

5. Here's how: Preheat the oven to 350°F (180°C). Line a 13 x 18-inch rimmed baking sheet with a silicone baking mat or parchment paper and brush with Pan Goo.

6. In a medium bowl, whisk together the cake flour, cocoa powder, coarse salt, and baking soda. Set aside.

7. Separate the eggs, placing the whites into the bowl of your electric mixer and the yolks in a large bowl.

8. Whisk the yolks with ½ cup (106 grams) of granulated sugar until they're light and fluffy, then whisk in the buttermilk, oil, vanilla, and espresso powder, followed by the flour mixture.

9. Using the electric mixer, whip the egg whites on medium speed until frothy. Slowly shake in the remaining ½ cup (106 grams) of granulated sugar while gradually increasing the mixer speed to high and continue whipping until soft peaks form. Stir about one third of the egg whites into the batter to lighten it, then gently, but effectively, fold in the remaining whites in two additions. Spread the batter into the prepared pan using an offset spatula.

10. Bake until the cake is firm and springs back to the touch, 12 to 14 minutes.

(continued)

11. Meanwhile, spread a clean, lint-free kitchen towel on your counter and dust it liberally with cocoa powder. As soon as the cake comes out of the oven, run a knife around the edges of the pan to loosen it, then flip it out of the pan onto the towel. Remove the baking mat or parchment paper and dust the cake with more cocoa. Starting at one of the short ends, roll the cake along with the towel into a log. This will make it easier to roll up around the filling later. Let the cake cool completely.

12. Carefully unroll the cake. I hope it hasn't cracked, but it happens sometimes. At the end of the day, it doesn't really matter. Briefly stir the caramel filling to loosen it, then spread it over the cake, leaving about a ½-inch border around the edges. Scatter the banana slices evenly over the filling and then reroll the cake. You can use the towel as a sort of a sling to shimmy the cake onto a serving platter, seam side down. Refrigerate until firm, which will take at least an hour or two.

13. To make the glaze, place the chocolate in a small heatproof bowl. Heat the cream in a small saucepan over low heat until bubbles form just around the edges, but do not let it boil. Pour the cream over the chocolate and let it sit for a minute or so to soften, then vigorously stir with a rubber spatula until a smooth ganache forms. Pour it over the top and sides of the roulade.

14. Let the ganache set, then garnish with flaky sea salt. Serve chilled or at cool room temperature.

STORAGE

The assembled cake will keep in the refrigerator, loosely covered, for up to 3 days.

GARNISHING GANACHE

Because salt attracts moisture, it can be a temperamental garnish for glazed cakes if you don't nail the timing. Too warm and the salt will dissolve; too cool and it won't stick. If you plan to assemble this cake well before your guests arrive, go ahead and refrigerate the glazed cake without garnishing. Then remove the cake and let it sit at room temperature for 30 minutes or so until the ganache softens before sprinkling with sea salt.

MAMEY CHEESECAKE

| MAKES 12 TO 14 SERVINGS | EASY | OVERNIGHT |
| SPECIAL EQUIPMENT: 9-INCH SPRINGFORM PAN |

Mamey, sometimes called *sapote*, is a tropical fruit that looks like what might happen if an avocado and a coconut got together with a sweet potato. The flavor is subtly reminiscent of persimmon and honey. Ripe fruit should give slightly when gently pressed but not bruise easily. Look for it in the summer and early fall at Latin American and specialty produce markets.

I've found that the secret to keeping a cheesecake from cracking is in the cooling. When the cake comes out of the oven, let it linger in the water bath for about 30 minutes, then transfer it to a wire rack to let it slowly cool to room temperature. Refrigerate well—at least 6 hours—before removing it from the pan.

FOR THE CRUST

graham crackers	12	186 grams
unsalted butter, melted	3 tablespoons	42 grams
honey	3 tablespoons	60 grams
coarse salt	1 pinch	1 pinch

FOR THE CHEESECAKE BATTER

firm-ripe mamey flesh (see page 108), packed	1 cup	260 grams
cream cheese, softened	4 cups (32 ounces)	904 grams
granulated sugar	1¼ cups	265 grams
honey	2 tablespoons	40 grams
ancho chile powder	¾ teaspoon	2.7 grams
coarse salt	1 pinch	1 pinch
large eggs	4	4

FOR THE HONEY-WHIPPED YOGURT

plain whole-milk Greek yogurt	1½ cups	375 grams
honey	3 tablespoons	60 grams
ancho chile powder (see page 73), for serving		

(continued)

1. Start off with the crust. Preheat the oven to 350°F (180°C) with a rack in the center position. Securely wrap the outside of a 9-inch springform pan with two layers of heavy-duty foil to create a water barrier.

2. Pulse the graham crackers in a food processor until they form coarse crumbs, then process until very fine, about 1 minute. Add the butter, honey, and salt and process until the mixture is evenly moistened. Press the crust into the bottom of the prepared pan, using a small flat-bottomed measuring scoop to firmly pack it into place.

3. Place the pan on a rimmed baking sheet and bake for about 12 minutes, until the crust is fragrant and golden and the surface is dry to the touch. (This is called "blind baking." See below.) Remove the pan from the oven and let it cool slightly while you make the cheesecake batter.

4. Reduce the oven temperature to 325°F (170°C) and bring a large kettle of water to a boil. In the bowl of the food processor, pulse the mamey flesh until a smooth puree forms, about 1 minute. Add the cream cheese, sugar, honey, chile powder, and a generous pinch of salt and process until completely homogenous. Scrape the sides of the bowl with a rubber spatula. Add the eggs, one at a time, processing well after each.

5. Pour the batter over the crust and smooth the top with a small offset spatula. Place the pan in the center of a large roasting pan and transfer to the oven. Carefully fill the roasting pan with enough hot water to come about halfway up the side of the pan—but no higher than the foil, lest there be a soggy bottom. Nobody likes a soggy bottom.

6. Bake for about 70 minutes, until only the center jiggles when the cake is gently shaken. Transfer the roasting pan to a wire rack and let the cake cool in the hot water for about 30 minutes. Remove the pan from the water bath and let it cool on the wire rack to room temperature, then refrigerate for at least 6 hours or overnight. Carefully remove the collar of the springform pan just before serving.

7. Whisk together the Greek yogurt and honey. To serve, dollop slices of cheesecake with the tangy topping and sprinkle with ancho chile powder.

STORAGE

The cake will keep, loosely covered, in the refrigerator for up to 3 days.

MAKING DO

If you can't find fresh mamey, it's fine to use frozen in this recipe. Let the thawed pulp drain on paper towels for a few minutes before adding it to the food processor. An equal amount of fresh mango makes a nice substitute, too.

PERFECT CRUST

Sometimes a graham cracker crust will bubble up a bit during blind baking, the process of prebaking a crust without any filling. If this happens to you, use the bottom of a measuring scoop to flatten out the crust while it is still hot, then return it to the oven for a minute or two to set.

STRAWBERRY FOOLS

| MAKES ABOUT 12 INDIVIDUAL FOOLS | EASY |

Juicy summer berries, a decadent custard, and mounds of whipped cream soften the crumbled ladyfingers. A trifle, but not a token.

You can use store-bought ladyfingers in a pinch.

FOR THE MACERATED STRAWBERRIES

strawberries, hulled and cut into halves and quarters	2 pounds	908 grams
granulated sugar, to taste	⅓ cup	71 grams
coarse salt	1 pinch	1 pinch
freshly ground black pepper	1 pinch	1 pinch
orange liqueur, such as Triple Sec, optional	2 tablespoons	30 milliliters

FOR ASSEMBLY

heavy cream	1½ cups	375 milliliters
crème fraîche	¼ cup	60 grams
confectioners' sugar, to taste	¼ cup	28 grams
pure vanilla extract	1 tablespoon	15 milliliters
Ladyfingers (page 227)	1 recipe	1 recipe
chilled Pastry Cream (page 234)	1 recipe	1 recipe

1. Macerate the strawberries: In a large bowl, combine the strawberries, granulated sugar, salt, pepper, and orange liqueur, stirring gently to coat the berries evenly without them breaking down. Refrigerate if you plan to let them sit for more than a few hours.

2. In a large bowl, whip the cream with the crème fraîche, confectioners' sugar, and vanilla until it forms soft peaks, about 3 minutes, depending on the shape of your forearms. Refrigerate until you're ready to assemble, up to 4 hours.

3. Strain the berries, reserving the syrup that they produced. Crumble 1 or 2 ladyfingers into the bottom of a small glass and drizzle with strawberry syrup. Spoon a heaping 2 tablespoons (30 milliliters) of pastry cream on top. Scatter about ¼ cup (34 grams) of strawberries on top of the pastry cream. Casually place another ladyfinger in the glass and dollop with the tangy whipped cream. Repeat with the remaining ingredients to make 12 servings. Serve chilled.

STORAGE

The fools can be assembled and chilled well in advance of serving, but they won't look as nice as ones that are freshly made.

KEY LIME CAKE

| MAKES 8 TO 10 SERVINGS | INTERMEDIATE | OVERNIGHT |
| SPECIAL EQUIPMENT: INSTANT-READ OR CANDY THERMOMETER, KITCHEN TORCH |

I don't know if you've ever squeezed a Key lime. It's a pain in the ass, but the flavor hiding in the modicum of juice you'll recover more than makes up for the struggle. You know what it tastes like; I know you know the pie. It's summer. Beachy. Floral. Have you ever rubbed your fingers across a wicker armrest and got lost in the undulating cords like waves?

FOR THE KEY LIME FILLING

Key lime juice (from about 1 pound/454 grams Key limes; see page 114)	½ cup	125 milliliters
large egg yolks	4	4
sweetened condensed milk	1 can (14 ounces)	397 grams
coarse salt	1 pinch	1 pinch
cornstarch	2 tablespoons	16 grams
cream cheese, cut into smallish pieces	1 cup (8 ounces)	226 grams

FOR THE SOAKER

granulated sugar	¼ cup	53 grams
Key lime juice (from about ½ pound/227 grams Key limes)	¼ cup	62 milliliters

FOR ASSEMBLY

Perfect Chiffon Cake (page 228), baked in two 8 x 2-inch round pans, cooled	1 recipe	1 recipe
coarsely crumbled graham crackers (from about 4 crackers)	½ cup	62 grams
large egg whites	4	4
granulated sugar	1 cup	212 grams

(continued)

1. Do yourself a favor and make the filling the night before you plan to assemble this cake. Have a fine-mesh sieve and a large bowl on standby near the stove. Squeeze every last drop of juice from the limes and combine in a small saucepan with the yolks, condensed milk, salt, and cornstarch. Whisk everything together until it's nice and smooth, and then set over medium heat. Don't stop whisking.

2. Reduce the temperature a bit as the mixture thickens dramatically and keep whisking as it boils for 2 minutes, being especially careful to keep the edges of the pot from scorching. It's not going to be a rolling boil like when you make a pot of pasta; it's more like geysers of steam breaking across the surface—watch out, they're hot!

3. Strain the mixture through the fine-mesh sieve into the bowl and stir gently with a rubber spatula to let off some of the steam. Add the cream cheese, one or two pieces at a time, and stir until all of it has been incorporated. Place a piece of plastic film or wax paper directly on the surface of the custard to prevent a skin from forming and refrigerate until firm, at least 4 hours, preferably overnight.

4. Make the lime soaker by stirring the sugar into the juice until it's dissolved. Set aside.

5. It's showtime. Use a serrated knife to trim the domes from the tops of the cakes and slice each in half horizontally to create four layers (see page 247). Place one layer on a serving platter and brush the top with about 2 tablespoons (30 milliliters) of the soaker. Stir the lime filling briefly to loosen it, then use a small offset spatula to spread about one third of the filling over the cake, getting it right up to the edge. Scatter a third of the graham cracker crumbs over the filling and top with another layer of cake. Continue assembling in this manner with the remaining filling and cake layers (see page 247). Slide a long wooden skewer vertically through the center of the cake if it feels wobbly. Chill the assembled cake until you're ready to make the meringue.

6. To make a Swiss meringue, place the egg whites and sugar in the heatproof bowl of an electric mixer. Set the bowl over a pan of gently simmering water and heat, whisking occasionally, until the sugar is dissolved and the mixture reads 160°F (71°C) on a thermometer, or is hot enough to hurt when you stick a finger into it. Transfer the bowl to the mixer and whip on high speed until firm peaks form, about 5 minutes.

7. Remove the skewer from the chilled cake and dollop the meringue on top, piling it high.* Gently brown the meringue with a kitchen torch. Serve at cool room temperature.

STORAGE

The cake can be stored, loosely covered, in the refrigerator for up to 2 days.

---

* Dolly Parton is often quoted thus: "The higher the hair, the closer to God." Same for meringues.

MAKING DO

If Key limes are unavailable, you can substitute equal parts lemon and lime juice.

HUMMINGBIRD LAYER CAKE

| MAKES 10 SERVINGS | EASY | OVERNIGHT |

This is the motherlode of modern fruitcakes, packed with sweet tropical ingredients. I spice mine up with a touch of mace, which helps to open up the flavor into something more robust than simply sweet. The Tangy Cream Cheese Frosting seals the deal.

FOR THE CAKE LAYERS

Pan Goo (page 224), for greasing the pan		
all-purpose flour	3 cups	426 grams
baking powder	2 teaspoons	6 grams
ground cinnamon	1 teaspoon	2.5 grams
coarse salt	1 teaspoon	3 grams
baking soda	½ teaspoon	3 grams
ground allspice	½ teaspoon	1 gram
ground mace (see page 77)	¼ teaspoon	1.2 grams
neutral oil, such as safflower	1 cup	250 milliliters
large eggs	3	3
granulated sugar	1 cup	212 grams
firmly packed light brown sugar	1 cup	212 grams
pure vanilla extract	1 teaspoon	5 milliliters
very ripe bananas, mashed	2	240 grams
very finely diced fresh pineapple	1 cup	210 grams
unsweetened shredded coconut, lightly toasted	1 cup	100 grams
chopped pecans, lightly toasted (see page 18)	1 cup	110 grams

FOR ASSEMBLY

Tangy Cream Cheese Frosting (page 230)	2 recipes	2 recipes

(continued)

1. Preheat the oven to 325°F (170°C) with a rack in the center position. Lightly brush two 8 x 2-inch round cake pans with Pan Goo and line the bottoms with parchment paper. This is a sticky cake, so the parchment really is important here.

2. In a medium bowl, whisk together the flour, baking powder, cinnamon, salt, baking soda, allspice, and mace. Set aside.

3. In a large bowl, whisk the oil, eggs, both sugars, vanilla, mashed bananas, pineapple, and coconut thoroughly to combine. The mixture will become thick and creamy and will lighten to an almost golden color because of the pineapple. Switch to a rubber spatula and gently stir in the dry ingredients, adding about one third of the mixture at a time. Gently fold in the pecans.

4. Divide the batter between the prepared pans, filling each about halfway, and tap firmly on the counter to dislodge any large air bubbles.

5. Bake the cakes until they are golden brown and firm to the touch and a cake tester inserted into the center comes out clean, about 55 minutes.

6. Transfer the pans to a wire rack. Allow the cakes to rest in the pans for about 10 minutes, then invert them onto the rack to cool completely. And I do mean completely; in fact, you'll be greatly rewarded in both flavor and ease of assembly if, once the cakes are cool, you wrap them well and refrigerate overnight before proceeding.

7. Use a long serrated knife to trim the domes from the tops of the cakes, if necessary, then split each cake in half horizontally, creating four layers (see page 247). To assemble, place one layer, with the flattest side down, on a cake stand or serving platter and cover it with a generous cup (about 275 grams) of cream cheese frosting, spreading it evenly and to the edges with a small offset spatula.

8. Carefully place a second cake layer on top and repeat with another generous cup (about 275 grams) of frosting. Continue building the cake in this way, until all four layers are in place. If your kitchen is warm, it may be helpful to refrigerate the cake for 20 minutes or so at this point to keep things from sliding around. Then, use about 1 cup (275 grams) of frosting to crumb coat the cake (see page 247), then chill the cake until things feel solid, about 45 minutes.

9. Generously coat the cake with the remaining frosting, swooping and swirling yourself into hypnosis. If clean slices are your thing, refrigerate the cake for at least an hour and bring to a cool room temperature before serving.

STORAGE

The frosted cake can be kept in the refrigerator, loosely covered, for 3 or 4 days.

WORKING AHEAD

The steps to make this cake can easily be spread out over the course of a few days. The cakes can be baked and stored (well wrapped) in the refrigerator for up to 2 days before assembling, or frozen for up to 1 month. The frosting can be made ahead and stored in an airtight container in the refrigerator for up to 1 week and brought to room temperature before using.

PASSION FRUIT LIME PAVLOVA

| MAKES 10 TO 12 SERVINGS | EASY | OVERNIGHT |
| SPECIAL EQUIPMENT: INSTANT-READ OR CANDY THERMOMETER |

I've never been to Australia, but Australians seem to gravitate toward me. My time in New York has been peppered with them. I've never known an Australian to actually make a pavlova, but they do love talking about them.

I don't love talking, but I do love making pavlovas. No matter what you do they seem to impress. When passion fruit is in season I can think of no better topping because their acidity cuts through the sweetness of the meringue. It's a balancing act, if not a pirouette.

It was my friend Kieran who put it best: The perfect pav should be crispy on the outside and chewy in the center, and if you find someone who can accomplish that, marry them. Don't you want to be that person, too?

FOR THE MERINGUE

large egg whites	6	6
granulated sugar	1½ cups	318 grams
coarse salt	1 pinch	1 pinch
cornstarch	1 tablespoon	8 grams
cider vinegar	2 teaspoons	10 milliliters

FOR THE FILLING

best-quality white chocolate, finely chopped	2 ounces	57 grams
heavy cream	¼ cup	62 milliliters
lime Ginger Citrus Curd (page 244), chilled	1 recipe	1 recipe
ripe and wrinkly passion fruit	2 (about 3 ounces total)	85 grams

FOR FINISHING

heavy cream	1 cup	250 milliliters
vanilla bean, split lengthwise and seeds scraped out	1	1
finger limes, for garnish (see page 121)		

(continued)

1. It's crucial that you make the meringue the night before your party, as pavlovas take quite a long time to cool. Trace an 8-inch circle onto a piece of parchment paper. Flip the parchment over so the marking is on the underside and set it on a very flat 13 x 18-inch rimmed baking sheet. (The marking should be visible through the paper.) Preheat the oven to 300°F (150°C) with a rack in the lowest position.

2. In the heatproof bowl of an electric mixer, combine the egg whites, sugar, and salt. Set the bowl over a pan of gently simmering water and heat, whisking frequently, until the mixture reaches 160°F (71°C) on a thermometer.

3. Transfer the bowl to the mixer fitted with the whisk attachment. Whip on high speed until the meringue is stiff and glossy and just barely warm to the touch, about 5 minutes. Add the cornstarch and cider vinegar and whisk to combine.

4. Scrape the meringue into the center of the template and use a rubber spatula to spread it to the edge of the circle, leaving the pile as swoopy or as tidy as you like.

5. Pop the meringue into the oven and immediately reduce the temperature to 225°F (110°C). Bake for 90 minutes. Don't open the door. Turn off the oven and let the meringue cool completely overnight. I almost always forget to take it out of the oven in the morning.

6. To make the filling, combine the white chocolate and cream in a heatproof bowl. Set the bowl over a pan of simmering water and heat, stirring constantly with a rubber spatula, until the chocolate has just melted. Remove the bowl from the pan and allow it to cool until it's just warm to the touch, stirring occasionally, then stir it into the chilled lime curd. Refrigerate the filling until you're ready to assemble the pavlova, for up to 1 day.

7. To assemble, peel the meringue off the parchment paper and transfer to a serving platter. Use the back of a spoon to crack the top, creating a wide divot to contain the filling. Spoon the white chocolate and lime custard into the divot. Split the passion fruit in half and spoon the pulp on top of the custard, letting it drip and pool down the sides of the meringue. It's a little grotesque, and that's why it's cool.

8. In a large bowl, whip the cream with the vanilla seeds until it forms soft peaks. Spoon the whipped cream over the pavlova. Garnish with finger lime pearls and serve immediately, using a sharp knife to slice into wedges.

FINGER LIMES

Finger limes, or caviar limes, are a special citrus native to Australia. They have a wonderful flavor—floral and just sweet enough to eat. Best of all, they're fun! Break them crosswise and squeeze the pearls (technically they're globular juice vesicles) into a bowl or directly into your mouth. If you can't get your hands on any finger limes, you can mist the assembled pav with a spritz of fresh lime juice instead.

SUMMER BERRY SHORTCAKES

| MAKES 6 SHORTCAKES | EASY |

These are the flakiest shortcakes I know how to make—the layers are so proud they practically split themselves in half if you so much as even look at them. My friend Betsy grew up in Georgia, and this is the same technique her mom, Terri, uses for her buttermilk biscuits. I've never visited Terri, but I've always imagined her house overflowing with those biscuits, the pillowcases stuffed with them.

I think that perfectly ripe berries need something acidic to really show off, so I've whipped up a tangy yogurt and cream situation to pair with them. The spoonful of jam melts into the cream, imbuing a mellowness only cooked fruit can provide.

FOR THE SHORTCAKES

all-purpose flour, plus additional for dusting	2¾ cups	391 grams
granulated sugar	½ cup	106 grams
baking powder	4 teaspoons	12 grams
coarse salt	1 teaspoon	3 grams
unsalted butter, cold and cut into ¼-inch pieces	¾ cup (1½ sticks)	170 grams
heavy cream, plus additional for brushing	1 cup	250 milliliters
sanding sugar, for sprinkling		

FOR SERVING

heavy cream	⅔ cup	166 milliliters
plain whole-milk Greek yogurt	⅔ cup	167 grams
pure vanilla extract	1 teaspoon	5 milliliters
Any Berry Jam (page 239)	½ cup	160 grams
mixed fresh berries	2 cups	270 grams

(continued)

1. In a medium bowl, whisk together the flour, granulated sugar, baking powder, and salt. Add the butter and toss the cubes through your fingers to break up the clumps that have stuck together, dispersing them throughout the mixture. Squeeze the butter between your fingers until each cube has been flattened into a small sheet. If you're lucky enough to have a kitchen window, stare blankly into the world outside while you consider every morsel. You're getting very sleepy.

2. Make a well in the center of the bowl and add the cream. Gently stir everything together with a wooden spoon until almost all the dry ingredients have been moistened but some dry patches remain. Turn the dough out onto a floured work surface and knead gently three or four times until the dough just begins to come together.

3. Press the dough into a rectangle about 6 x 8 inches. Using a bench scraper or an offset spatula to help, flip one half of the dough over the other so the short sides meet, then press the dough out again and repeat the folding process two more times. Finish by shaping the dough into a rectangle that's about 6 x 8 inches. Wrap the dough in wax paper or plastic film and refrigerate for at least 45 minutes or overnight.

4. Preheat the oven to 425°F (220°C) with a rack in the center position. Line a rimmed baking sheet with a silicone baking mat or parchment paper.

5. Using a sharp knife, trim about ¼ inch from each side of the dough rectangle, exposing all the lovely layers—this will help the shortcakes rise more evenly. Slice the dough in half lengthwise and in thirds crosswise, forming 6 shortcakes, and place the darlings about 2 inches apart on the sheet. Gather the scraps into a hideous little shortcake and bake them, too: cook's treat. Brush the tops with cream and sprinkle generously with sanding sugar.

6. Bake the shortcakes until they are puffed and golden brown around the edges and a toothpick inserted into a center comes out clean, about 22 minutes. Transfer to a wire rack to cool, but don't wait more than a couple of hours before serving.

7. In a large bowl, combine the cream, yogurt, and vanilla and whisk with vigor until soft, curvaceous peaks form. Just before serving, split the shortcakes in half and top with a spoonful of jam, a scattering of berries, and a dollop of the tangy whipped cream. Serve immediately.

CRANBERRY YULE LOG

| MAKES 12 TO 15 SERVINGS | ADVANCED | MULTIDAY |

Yule logs are dauntingly impressive but manageable when you break them down into steps. This is my favorite type of project because the payoff really outweighs the effort, especially if you begin making the components a few days in advance. Most of the individual steps can be accomplished in the evening without much fuss, leaving you with little to do but assemble and decorate the cake on the final day. Here's how I might go about it:

Day One, or even a week ahead: Make the Cranberry Jam.

Day Two: Make the Swiss Meringue Buttercream.

Day Three: Make the chocolate custard and refrigerate overnight. Pull the buttercream out of the refrigerator just before bed so that it's ready to use the next day.

Day Four, morning: Bake and cool the Perfect Chiffon Cake. Pull the chocolate custard out of the refrigerator to come to room temperature. Meanwhile, go for a walk in the park to see what real logs look like.

Day Four, early afternoon: Fill the cake with the Cranberry Jam and flavor the buttercream with the chocolate custard.

Day Four, midafternoon: Finish assembling and decorating the cake, then refrigerate it until your guests arrive, or even for a day or two.

FOR THE CHOCOLATE CUSTARD

unsweetened cocoa powder, preferably Dutch-processed	2 tablespoons	10 grams
cornstarch	1 tablespoon	8 grams
coarse salt	1 pinch	1 pinch
whole milk	½ cup	125 milliliters
best-quality dark chocolate, 70% to 80% cacao, finely chopped	3 ounces	85 grams

FOR ASSEMBLY

orange liqueur, such as Triple Sec	2 tablespoons	30 milliliters
Perfect Chiffon Cake (page 228), baked and cooled as a roulade	1 recipe	1 recipe
Cranberry Jam (page 242), chilled	¾ cup	225 grams

(continued)

Swiss Meringue Buttercream (page 233), room temperature	1 recipe	1 recipe
finely chopped pistachios, for garnish		

1. I think the best way to make a rich chocolate buttercream is with a custard base. Here's how: In a small saucepan, whisk together the cocoa powder, cornstarch, and salt. Add the milk, a little bit at a time, whisking to form a lump-free paste, then whisk in the rest of the milk until well combined.

2. Place the saucepan over medium heat, whisking constantly until the mixture thickens and begins to boil, about 4 minutes. Off heat, add in the chopped chocolate. Let it soften for about 1 minute, then stir vigorously with a rubber spatula to combine. Transfer to a heatproof bowl and press a piece of plastic film or wax paper onto the surface of the custard to prevent a skin from forming. Let cool to room temperature or refrigerate overnight. (Bring to room temperature before using.)

3. Next, assemble the cake. In a small bowl, stir the orange liqueur together with 1 tablespoon (15 milliliters) water. Gently unroll the cooled chiffon cake, trying as hard as you can not to crack it, but no one will ever know if you do. Brush the surface with the orange liqueur mixture, then use an offset spatula to spread a thin layer of the cranberry jam over the surface of the cake, leaving about a ½-inch border around the edges. Gently reroll the cake and transfer it to a serving platter, seam side down.

4. In the bowl of an electric mixer fitted with the paddle attachment, beat the Swiss meringue buttercream and cooled chocolate custard on low speed until combined, stopping occasionally to scrape down the sides of the bowl, about 2 minutes.

5. Use a sharp, serrated knife to trim about 1 inch from each end of the roulade. Use some chocolate buttercream to affix the trimmed pieces to the top and side of the roulade to create the look of cut-off branches. Refrigerate the cake until the frosting firmly holds the pieces in place, about 15 minutes.

6. Use a small offset spatula to frost the cake with the remaining chocolate buttercream, working back and forth lengthwise to create a gnarly, barky texture. If at any point the cake becomes difficult to work with, pop it back in the refrigerator for 15 minutes or so, until the frosting firms up. You can always layer more frosting on top of the bark to create more texture. We're making a French tree, not an Italian car.

7. When you're satisfied with the coverage and texture of the chocolate buttercream, refrigerate the cake for about 45 minutes, until the frosting is set.

8. Scatter a moss of finely chopped pistachios into the crevasses. Bring the cake to a cool room temperature before cutting crosswise into thin slices.

STORAGE

The assembled cake will keep for 2 or 3 days in the refrigerator, loosely covered.

COCONUT CIELO CAKE

| DAIRY-FREE | MAKES 8 TO 10 SERVINGS | INTERMEDIATE | OVERNIGHT |

Miles high and bursting with coconut, this is a cake worth celebrating. The slender shape and six—count them, six!—layers will impress anyone worth your time. But the time it takes to make it is less than it seems; spread out over a couple of days, this cake comes together more easily than you might expect. The hard part: stopping after only one slice.

FOR THE COCONUT FILLING

granulated sugar	1 cup	212 grams
unsweetened shredded coconut	¾ cup	75 grams
cornstarch	¼ cup	32 grams
coarse salt	½ teaspoon	1.5 grams
unsweetened coconut milk	1 can (13.5 ounces)	400 milliliters
large egg yolks	4	4
pure vanilla extract	1 tablespoon	15 milliliters
coconut oil, melted	1 tablespoon	14 grams

FOR THE COCONUT CAKE LAYERS

Pan Goo (page 224), for greasing the pan		
cake flour	2 cups	226 grams
unsweetened shredded coconut	1 cup	100 grams
granulated sugar, divided	1 cup	212 grams
baking powder	2 teaspoons	6 grams
coarse salt	1 teaspoon	3 grams
unsweetened coconut milk	½ cup	125 milliliters
large eggs, separated	4	4
pure vanilla extract	1 tablespoon	15 milliliters
coconut oil, melted	6 tablespoons	84 grams

(continued)

large egg whites	4	4
granulated sugar	1 cup	212 grams
freshly shaved coconut (see page 248), for garnish		

1. The coconut filling can be made up to 2 days in advance. In a small saucepan, combine the sugar, coconut, cornstarch, and salt and whisk to combine.

2. In a small bowl, whisk together the coconut milk, egg yolks, and vanilla.

3. Whisk the wet ingredients into the sugar mixture and set over medium heat, whisking frequently until the mixture thickens and starts to boil, about 6 minutes. Continue boiling the mixture, whisking constantly to keep it from scorching, for about 2 minutes, until very thick. Whisk in the coconut oil.

4. Pour the custard into a small heatproof bowl and press a piece of plastic film or wax paper directly on the surface to prevent a skin from forming. Refrigerate until firm, at least 2 hours or overnight.

5. To make the cake layers, preheat the oven to 350°F (180°C) with a rack in the center position. Brush three 6 x 2-inch round cake pans with Pan Goo.

6. In the bowl of a food processor, combine the cake flour, coconut, ½ cup (106 grams) of the sugar, the baking powder, and salt. Process the mixture until the coconut has been ground into a fairly fine powder, about 1 minute. In a medium bowl, whisk together the coconut milk, egg yolks, and vanilla. With the food processor running, stream the coconut oil through the feed tube, followed by the coconut milk mixture, processing until a smooth batter forms, about 1 minute. Scrape the batter into a large bowl and set aside.

7. Using an electric mixer fitted with the whisk attachment, whip the egg whites on medium speed until foamy. Gradually add the remaining ½ cup (106 grams) of sugar to the egg whites while increasing the mixer speed to high. Continue whipping until firm peaks form, about 2 minutes.

8. Stir about a third of the egg whites into the batter to lighten, then gently fold the remaining egg whites into the batter in two additions. Divide among the prepared cake pans, filling each about two thirds of the way to the top.

9. Bake until the cakes are firm to the touch and a cake tester inserted into each center comes out with moist crumbs, about 30 minutes.

10. Transfer the pans to wire racks. Let the cakes rest in the pans for about 10 minutes, then invert them onto the racks to cool completely. The cooled cakes can be stored in an airtight container overnight before assembling.

11. Use a sharp serrated knife to trim the domes from the tops of the cakes, then split each layer in half horizontally to create a total of 6 cake layers (see page 247). Stir the coconut filling to loosen.

12. Place one cake layer on a serving platter or rotating cake stand and cover with a heaping ⅓ cup (83 milliliters) of the coconut filling, using a small offset spatula to spread the filling right to the edge. Top with a second cake layer and continue assembling the cake, alternating layers of cake and filling, and ending with a cake layer with its flattest side up. The cake may be a bit wobbly at this point, so insert a long wooden

skewer all the way through the center, reaching to the bottom of the cake. Crumb coat the cake by thinly spreading any remaining filling on the outside of the cake, filling any gaps. Refrigerate until firm, about 2 hours, or even overnight.

13. To finish the cake, make a simple Swiss meringue: Combine the egg whites and sugar in the heatproof bowl of an electric mixer. Set the bowl over a pan of gently simmering water and heat the mixture, whisking occasionally, until the sugar dissolves and the egg whites are hot to the touch (about 160°F, 71°C), about 5 minutes. Transfer the bowl to the mixer and whip on high speed, using the whisk attachment, until a stiff, glossy meringue forms, about 4 minutes.

14. Use an offset spatula to spread the meringue over the top and sides of the cake. Garnish the top with freshly shaved coconut. Serve the cake at cool room temperature, using a sharp knife to cut slender slices. It's sort of a complicated serve.

STORAGE

Leftovers can be refrigerated, loosely covered, for up to 3 days. Meringues don't always enjoy refrigeration, so if you make the cake ahead of time, plan to frost it the day you serve it.

RASPBERRY DACQUOISE CAKE

| GLUTEN-FREE | MAKES 10 TO 12 SERVINGS | INTERMEDIATE | OVERNIGHT |

If you assemble this cake the morning of your party, the layers of dacquoise will have time to absorb some of the moisture from the mousseline filling. You'll end up with a mix of textures—spongy, crisp, and decadently rich. This is a time for small servings.

Because the dacquoise bakes at a low temperature and the cake is served chilled, it's a perfect treat for a summer evening.

FOR THE DACQUOISE LAYERS

finely ground almond flour	⅓ cup	33 grams
unsweetened cocoa powder, preferably Dutch-processed	1 tablespoon	5 grams
cornstarch	2 tablespoons	16 grams
ground cinnamon	1 teaspoon	2.5 grams
large egg whites	6	6
coarse salt	½ teaspoon	1.5 grams
granulated sugar	1 cup	212 grams
sliced almonds	¾ cup	79 grams

FOR THE RASPBERRY MOUSSELINE

Pastry Cream (page 234), still warm	1 recipe	1 recipe
unsalted butter, cool but pliable	1 cup (2 sticks)	226 grams
fresh raspberries	6 ounces	170 grams

FOR FINISHING

best-quality dark chocolate, preferably about 65% cacao, finely chopped	3 ounces	85 grams
heavy cream, divided	1 cup	250 milliliters
freshly grated nutmeg	1 pinch	1 pinch
confectioners' sugar	2 tablespoons	14 grams
fresh raspberries, for garnish	6 ounces	170 grams

1. Because dacquoise is really just a gussied-up meringue, it's crucial that you get everything ready before you start putting it together. Begin with the templates: Trace four 7-inch circles onto parchment sheets, two per sheet and at least 1 inch apart. Flip the parchment sheets over so the markings are on the underside and use them to line two 13 x 18-inch rimmed baking sheets. (The markings should be visible through the paper.) Preheat the oven to 250°F (130°C) with racks in the upper- and lower-third positions.

2. In a small bowl, whisk together the almond flour, cocoa powder, cornstarch, and cinnamon, and set aside. Have a coarse-mesh sieve, a large rubber spatula, and a small offset spatula waiting in the wings.

3. In the bowl of an electric mixer fitted with the whisk attachment, place the egg whites and salt together. Begin whipping on medium speed until the mixture is foamy, then slowly add the granulated sugar while gradually increasing the speed to medium-high. When all the sugar is in

(continued)

the bowl, increase the speed to high and whip until the mixture forms stiff—but not dry—peaks, about 2 minutes longer.

4. Sift about a third of the almond and cocoa powder mixture through the coarse-mesh sieve over the egg whites and fold gently with the large rubber spatula to combine. Begin adding another third of the dry mixture while the egg whites are still streaky, fold a bit, and then sift in the remaining dry ingredients. Continue folding until they have been incorporated.

5. Dollop the batter into the center of each template and spread with a small offset spatula to fill the marked circles. The edges don't need to be perfect; they just need to be charming. Scatter the sliced almonds evenly over the batter and get the pans directly into the oven. Do not pass go.

6. Bake the dacquoise for 2 hours, then turn the oven off and leave them inside to cool completely, preferably overnight.

7. The mousseline filling should be made with pastry cream that is just barely warm. Make a fresh batch following the instructions on page 234, then strain it directly into the bowl of an electric mixer. Using the paddle attachment, beat the hot pastry cream on medium speed for about 5 minutes, until it's no longer steaming and the outside of the bowl is warm but not hot.

8. Check the temperature by beating in 1 tablespoon (14 grams) of butter—it should dissolve into the pastry cream without melting; let the pastry cream continue to cool for another minute or two if the mixture appears greasy. Continue adding the butter, a few tablespoons at a time, beating well after each addition. When all the butter has been added, beat on medium-high speed for about 2 minutes, until it becomes a rich buttercream. Add the raspberries and continue beating until they have just broken down.

9. Transfer the mousseline filling to a pastry bag fitted with a ⅜-inch plain round tip, such as an Ateco 804, or don't.

10. Place one dacquoise layer on a serving platter and pipe or spread a third of the mousseline filling on top. Add another dacquoise and continue building the cake, as you do. Refrigerate the assembled cake while you make the glaze.

11. Place the chocolate in a small heatproof bowl. In a small saucepan, heat ⅓ cup (83 milliliters) of the cream with the nutmeg until bubbles form around the edge of the pan and the first wisps of steam begin to rise from the surface. Pour the hot cream over the chocolate and let it sit for about 1 minute to soften. Then, working outward from the center of the bowl, stir the cream and chocolate together with a rubber spatula until it transforms into a silky nutmeg ganache.

12. Let the mixture cool, stirring occasionally, until it forms a ribbon that disappears into itself after about 3 seconds when dropped from the rubber spatula. This could take 10 or 15 minutes in a warm kitchen.

13. Pour the ganache over the chilled cake, spreading it to the edge with an offset spatula and letting it drip over the sides. Refrigerate until the ganache has set, 15 minutes or up to 1 day.

14. Just before serving, whip the remaining ⅔ cup (167 milliliters) of cream with the confectioners' sugar until soft peaks form. Dollop the cream on top of the cake and garnish with raspberries. Serve chilled or at cool room temperature, using a sharp knife to slice into wedges.

STORAGE

The assembled cake can be kept in the refrigerator, loosely covered, for about a day. The dacquoise will continue to soften as it sits; maybe you're into that. I am.

HORCHATA AND ROASTED PLUM SORBET CAKE

| GLUTEN-FREE, DAIRY-FREE | MAKES 8 TO 10 SERVINGS | INTERMEDIATE | OVERNIGHT |
| SPECIAL EQUIPMENT: NUT MILK BAG, ICE CREAM MACHINE, 10 X 5-INCH LOAF PAN |

By the middle of August, we couldn't remember how it felt not to stick together. Knees and elbows pasted. At night we'd climb to the roof with our five-gallon buckets, splashing our feet as we watered the strawberries. We lit candles under gibbous moons.

You said once that you don't need to tell me that you love me because you show me every day. I let it go, because I, too, am better at feeling without talking. *Y porque todavía no sé las palabras, aunque estoy tratando de aprender.*

I made you this to remind you of home. *Ciruelas tan rojas como mi corazón, solo un poco más frías.*

FOR THE ROASTED PLUMS

firm-ripe red or black plums, pitted and quartered	6 (about 1¼ pounds total)	567 grams
granulated sugar	6 tablespoons	80 grams
coarse salt	1 pinch	1 pinch

FOR THE HORCHATA SORBET

white jasmine rice, uncooked	1½ cups	267 grams
unsweetened coconut milk	1 can (13.5 ounces)	400 milliliters
granulated sugar	1 cup	212 grams
corn syrup (see page 136)	3 tablespoons	63 grams
ground cinnamon	1 tablespoon	7.5 grams
coarse salt	½ teaspoon	1.5 grams

FOR ASSEMBLY

coarsely crumbled graham crackers (gluten-free, if desired)	12	186 grams

(continued)

1. Preheat the oven to 350°F (180°C) with a rack in the center position.

2. Toss the plums with the sugar and salt and arrange them, skin sides down, on a rimmed baking sheet. Roast until the skins loosen and the flesh is very soft, 10 to 15 minutes. Toss them around a bit toward the end. Scrape the plums and their juice into a medium heatproof bowl, then cover and refrigerate overnight.

3. In another medium bowl, combine the rice with 2 cups (500 milliliters) cold water. Cover and refrigerate overnight, too.

4. The next day, with clean hands, remove and discard the skins from the plums. Use a fork or a potato masher to break up any large chunks of plum that didn't fall apart in the oven, but leave some pieces for texture. Keep chilled.

5. Transfer the rice and water to a blender and puree on high speed until the rice is almost completely dissolved, 2 to 3 minutes. Strain the mixture through a nut milk bag into a large bowl and squeeze the bag to recover as much liquid as possible. Discard the solids (if you've used a high-speed blender there will be almost none).

6. Return the rice milk to the blender. Add the coconut milk, sugar, corn syrup, cinnamon, and salt. Puree on high speed until the sugar dissolves, about 30 seconds. Chill the sorbet base for at least 1 hour or overnight.

7. While you wait, line a 10 x 5-inch loaf pan with a double layer of plastic film or freezer paper, leaving about 2 inches overhanging the sides of the pan to create a sling. Spread about a third of the roasted plums and their juice in the bottom of the pan and scatter a quarter of the graham cracker pieces on top. Place in the coldest part of your freezer for at least 1 hour. This serves the dual purposes of prechilling the pan and guaranteeing you'll find a spot for it in the freezer later.

8. Freeze the sorbet base in an ice cream machine according to the manufacturer's instructions. Be prepared to work quickly to assemble the cake the moment the sorbet is ready.

9. Spread about a third of the horchata sorbet into the prechilled pan. Scatter another third of the plums and quarter of the graham crackers on top of the sorbet, then quickly layer with another third of sorbet, the remaining plums, and another quarter of the graham crackers. Top with the final third of sorbet and the remaining graham crackers. Immediately transfer to the freezer and chill for at least 8 hours, preferably overnight.

10. When you're ready to serve, use the sling to pull the cake out of the mold. It may be helpful to let the cake warm up slightly if it appears to be firmly stuck in place. (You can dip the pan in a bowl of warm water if need be.) Invert the cake onto a serving platter and remove the sling. Use a sharp knife to cut crosswise into slices and serve immediately.

STORAGE

Store in the freezer, wrapped, for up to 2 weeks.

UNDERSTANDING

There's an ingredient in the list you may not expect and may object to on principle. Sorbet is a delicate balance of chemistry and physics, and the corn syrup in this recipe is there for a reason: Sugar plays a key role by lowering the freezing point of the liquid to create a creamy texture. Corn syrup, which is highly viscous and less sweet than sugar, helps to keep sorbets from becoming icy. The amount in this recipe works out to be less than a teaspoon per serving and is worth the sacrifice.

UME-SHISO WATERMELON FROZEN YOGURT CAKE

Shiso, a relative of the mint plant, is a staple of Japanese cuisine and can be found in two varieties: red and green. The red type (aka-jiso) is used in the production of pickled plums, called umeboshi, a common condiment. When mixed with salt, sugar, and other spices, dried red shiso leaves can be enjoyed as furikake, or rice seasoning, which is also a wonderful accompaniment to fresh fruit. Some ume-shiso furikake includes the juice from the pickled plums; this is my favorite style. Furikake is available at Japanese markets and online.

FOR THE CAKE

Pan Goo (page 224), for greasing the pan		
all-purpose flour	½ cup	71 grams
baking powder	¼ teaspoon	0.8 gram
coarse salt	¼ teaspoon	0.8 gram
large egg	1	1
granulated sugar	⅓ cup	71 grams
neutral oil, such as safflower	4 teaspoons	20 milliliters
pure vanilla extract	1 teaspoon	5 milliliters

FOR THE WATERMELON FROZEN YOGURT

peeled, seeded, and cubed watermelon, from half a small watermelon	2 pounds (about 7 cups)	907 grams
granulated sugar	¾ cup	159 grams
corn syrup (see page 136)	⅓ cup	113 grams
plain whole-milk yogurt (not Greek style)	1 cup	230 grams
ume-shiso furikake (prepared dried red shiso leaves)	4 teaspoons	8 grams
fresh red shiso leaves, for garnish		

(continued)

SHOWSTOPPERS

1. The cake should be baked and cooled before you begin on the frozen yogurt. Preheat the oven to 350°F (180°C) with a rack in the center position. Line a 7-inch springform pan with a piece of parchment paper and brush with Pan Goo.

2. In a small bowl, whisk together the flour, baking powder, and salt.

3. In a medium bowl, whisk together the egg, sugar, oil, and vanilla.

4. Stir the dry ingredients into the wet with a rubber spatula, mixing just until combined. Scrape the batter into the prepared pan and smooth the top with a small offset spatula. Bake the cake until the center springs back to the touch, about 12 minutes. Allow the cake to cool completely in the pan.

5. Remove the cake from the pan and peel off the parchment paper. Wash and dry the pan, then slip the cake back inside. Place in the coldest part of your freezer for at least 1 hour or overnight.

6. To make the frozen yogurt base, combine the watermelon, sugar, and corn syrup in a blender. Puree on high speed until smooth, about 1 minute. Add the yogurt and ume-shiso furikake and puree until combined, about 30 seconds longer. Cover and refrigerate the mixture until well chilled, at least 2 hours or overnight.

7. Briefly stir the frozen yogurt base to recombine any liquid that has risen to the surface, then freeze in an ice cream machine according to the manufacturer's directions.

8. As soon as the frozen yogurt is ready, spoon it on top of the cake in the springform pan. Be quick about it so that it doesn't melt, but also be careful to distribute it evenly and avoid creating unsightly air pockets. Immediately rush the assembled cake back into the freezer to solidify for at least 6 hours or overnight.

9. When you're ready to serve the cake, release the latch on the springform pan and gently pry open the collar. Slip the cake out of the collar and use a thin, sturdy spatula to transfer the cake to a serving platter. Garnish with fresh shiso leaves. Use a sharp knife to slice the cake into wedges to serve.

STORAGE

The assembled cake can be stored, well wrapped, in the freezer for up to 1 week.

GUAVA CREPE CAKE

| MAKES ABOUT 10 SERVINGS | INTERMEDIATE | OVERNIGHT |
| SPECIAL EQUIPMENT: 8-INCH NONSTICK SKILLET, HEATPROOF BRUSH |

Layer upon layer of paper-thin crepes, stacked with tangy guava pastry cream. Who knew something so extravagant could come together without even turning on the oven?

FOR THE CREPES

whole milk	2⅔ cups	666 milliliters
large eggs	4 whole, plus 4 yolks	4 whole, plus 4 yolks
all-purpose flour	1⅓ cups	189 grams
granulated sugar	⅓ cup	71 grams
coarse salt	½ teaspoon	1.5 grams
pure vanilla extract	1 tablespoon	15 milliliters
unsalted butter, melted and cooled, plus additional melted butter for frying	5 tablespoons	71 grams

FOR THE FILLING AND FINISHING

guava paste, cut into ½-inch pieces	1¾ cups (1 pound)	454 grams
Pastry Cream (page 234), chilled	1 recipe	1 recipe
best-quality white chocolate, melted and cooled	6 ounces	170 grams
heavy cream, divided	1½ cups	275 milliliters
white chocolate curls (see page 248), for garnish		

1. To make the crepe batter, combine all the ingredients in a blender and process on high speed until there are no lumps or dry spots, which will take about 1 minute. Scrape down the sides of the blender and pulse a few times, for kicks. Refrigerate the batter overnight or for at least 2 hours. It will separate as it rests, so pulse the batter a few more times to recombine just before making the crepes.

2. Settle in because it's going to be a good 35 minutes of frying crepes one at a time. It helps to get a little station set up. Melt about 3 tablespoons (42 grams) of butter and keep it warm in a small bowl. You'll need a nonstick skillet, preferably ceramic, with a flat area that's about 8 inches across. Grab a heatproof brush for the butter, a ⅓ cup (83 milliliter) measuring scoop, a long-handled spoon, a small offset

(continued) **141**

spatula, a couple of large plates, and tongs, if you insist.

3. Heat the skillet over medium until water droplets sizzle when they land, then brush with a thin coating of melted butter. Stir the batter and fill the measuring scoop almost, but not quite, to the top. Hold the pan away from the heat and pour the batter into the center, tilting and swirling the pan so that it forms a thin, even layer across the bottom. Listen to that sizzle! Return the pan to the heat and cook for about 1 minute, until the surface is dry and the edges are brown.

4. Use the offset spatula to gently lift the edge of the crepe that's farthest away from you. With nimble fingers, or tongs, if you just can't take the heat, grab the crepe about 1 inch from the edge, pinching with both thumbs and forefingers, and then boldly lift and flip it toward you. Continue cooking for 10 to 15 seconds, then slide the crepe out of the pan onto the plate.

5. Brush the pan with butter and start all over again, stirring the crepe batter as you work to keep it from separating. Pile the crepes on top of one another; I promise they won't stick together. Let them cool completely. Some will be total disasters, but not to worry; the batter makes about 20 crepes and you'll need only 15 or so for the cake. The rest are for snacking.

6. To make the filling, mash the guava paste in a large bowl until it's mostly smooth and only a smattering of pea-size morsels remains. Stir the chilled pastry cream into the guava paste with a rubber spatula, mixing until it's well combined, then stir in the white chocolate.

7. In a large bowl, whip ¾ cup (138 milliliters) of the cream to stiff peaks, then gently fold into the guava filling using a rubber spatula.

8. Place one crepe on a serving platter and spread about ¼ cup (62 milliliters) of the filling over the surface, leaving about a ¼-inch border. Layer with another crepe and more filling and continue building the cake until you run out of either crepes or filling, saving the most beautiful crepe in the land for the top.

9. Refrigerate the assembled cake for at least 8 hours. Just before serving, whip the remaining ¾ cup (138 milliliters) of cream to firm peaks and dollop on top of the cake. Garnish with white chocolate curls, and use a sharp knife to cut none-too-narrow wedges that won't topple over when you serve them. Don't try to take it on the subway.

STORAGE

The assembled cake can be stored, loosely covered, in the refrigerator for up to 2 days.

THOUGHTS ON TRANSPORTING A DELICATE CAKE BY NEW YORK CITY TRANSIT ON THE FIRST WEEKEND OF SUMMER:

It was

The Big Ooze

The Uptown Drip

The Slick Slider

The Slippery Slip

The Subway Slimer

The Summertime Shift

Looked like a dog

But they said it was delish

KIWI AND GOLDENBERRY SARATOGA TORTE

| MAKES ABOUT 10 SERVINGS | EASY | OVERNIGHT |

Saratoga torte is pavlova's hipster cousin. Both come from Down Under, but while pavlova's meringue is prim and proper, the addition of crumbled ladyfingers gives the Saratoga torte a chewier, cakier texture. You can use store-bought ladyfingers, if you prefer.

large egg whites	4	4
coarse salt	½ teaspoon	1.5 grams
superfine sugar, divided	¾ cup, plus 1 tablespoon	159 grams, plus 13 grams
freshly squeezed lemon juice (from 1 lemon)	1 tablespoon	15 milliliters
crumbled Ladyfingers (page 227), from about 12 crispy cookies	1½ cups	100 grams
Meyer lemon Ginger Citrus Curd (page 244)	1 recipe	1 recipe
kiwis, 1 cut into ½-inch pieces, the other 2 thinly sliced	3	390 grams
heavy cream	¾ cup	187 milliliters
fresh goldenberries	½ cup	81 grams

1. Preheat the oven to 350°F (180°C) with a rack in the center position. Line a 13 x 18-inch rimmed baking sheet with parchment and set aside.
2. In the bowl of an electric mixer fitted with the whisk attachment, whip the egg whites and salt on medium speed for 1 minute or so, until frothy. Shake ¾ cup (159 grams) of the superfine sugar into the whipping egg whites, about 1 tablespoon (13 grams) at a time, while slowly increasing the mixer speed to high. Continue whipping until very stiff peaks form, about 4 minutes. Quickly whisk in the lemon juice, then fold in the ladyfingers.
3. Dollop the meringue onto the prepared baking sheet, forming a circle about 6 inches across.
4. Place the meringue in the oven and immediately reduce the temperature to 225°F (110°C). Bake for 1 hour, then turn off the oven and let the meringue cool inside overnight.
5. To assemble, spread the curd across the torte and scatter the chopped kiwis across the top.
6. In a medium bowl, use a large whisk to whip the cream and remaining 1 tablespoon (13 grams) superfine sugar to soft peaks, about 1 minute. Dollop on top of the curd.
7. Arrange the sliced kiwis and goldenberries on top of the cream. Use a sharp knife to slice into wedges and serve at once.

MAKING DO

If fresh goldenberries are unavailable, substitute with a smattering of your favorite fruit.

ALL RISE

The invention of chemical leaveners like baking powder and soda caused a sea change in the baking industry. No longer reliant on the fragility of beaten eggs or the fickleness of yeast, bakers were able to standardize their products with exacting precision. It was an important discovery, but there is an authenticity that comes from baking with yeast that cannot be mimicked by any other means. It's not just about creating lift; yeast changes dough as it ferments by strengthening the gluten network and adding complex flavor compounds.

Since yeast is a living organism, it is by nature inexact, its behavior not completely predictable. You have to work with yeast; it doesn't work for you. But learning to harness its strength is one of the most satisfying skills a baker can master. The key is to be observant and to use all your senses to catalog how the dough changes over time.

Yeast's transformative power is as close to alchemy as you can get—I defy you not to swoon at the smell of just-risen dough or a yeasted cake fresh from the oven.

150	BLOOD ORANGE BEE-STING CAKE
154	BOURBON PEACH KUGELHOPF
157	BIM'S YEAST CAKE
160	CINNAMON RAISIN BUNS
163	CONCORD GRAPE FOCACCIA
167	PANETTONE TROPICALE
172	ROSCA DE REYES
177	STOLLEN
180	NECTARINE KUCHEN
183	CHOCOLATE ORANGE BABKA

BLOOD ORANGE BEE-STING CAKE

A family of wild cats lives in our backyard. They're cute enough, but they scream like banshees on warm nights, and I can only imagine what they're up to. When I try to get their attention, they scurry into the neighbor's thicket, but every now and then I catch one curled up sweetly, oblivious to the world outside its sunbeam. House cats, nearly. My friend Shira says they're a menace, but who am I to judge?

Hang in there, baby.

I'm trying to tell you the secret to making the softest, cakiest yeasted dough, and that's to let it come together almost entirely of its own accord. Like those cats, this cake won't come when called, but step back and watch as the dough transforms from a sticky mess into a tidy ball as it rises. It bakes itself into a little pillow, the perfect complement to the creamy blood orange filling—sweet, bitter, and bright.

FOR THE FILLING

granulated sugar	¼ cup	53 grams
cornstarch	2 tablespoons	16 grams
coarse salt	¼ teaspoon	0.8 gram
large egg yolks	3	3
freshly squeezed blood orange juice (from 2 blood oranges)	½ cup	125 milliliters
freshly squeezed lemon juice (from 1 lemon)	2 tablespoons	30 milliliters
unsalted butter	4 tablespoons (½ stick)	57 grams
orange liqueur, such as Triple Sec	1 tablespoon	15 milliliters
mascarpone cheese	½ cup	113 grams

whole milk, about 110°F (43°C)	½ cup	125 milliliters
honey	3 tablespoons	60 grams
pure vanilla extract	1 teaspoon	5 milliliters
instant yeast (see page 10)	1 teaspoon	3 grams
large eggs	1 whole, plus 1 yolk	1 whole, plus 1 yolk
all-purpose flour, plus additional for dusting	2 cups	284 grams
coarse salt	1 teaspoon	3 grams
finely grated blood orange zest (from 1 blood orange)	2 teaspoons	4 grams
unsalted butter, very soft, plus additional for the pan	5 tablespoons	71 grams
blood orange, very thinly sliced	1	100 grams
confectioners' sugar, for dusting		

freshly squeezed blood orange juice (from 1 blood orange)	¼ cup	62 milliliters
honey	¼ cup	80 grams

1. Make the filling first, even 2 days ahead. In a small saucepan, whisk the granulated sugar, cornstarch, salt, and egg yolks to combine. Add the blood orange and lemon juices and whisk until no lumps remain. Cook the mixture over medium heat until it thickens and begins to boil, whisking constantly. Continue whisking for 2 minutes.

2. Strain through a fine-mesh sieve into a heatproof bowl and stir in the butter, a little bit at a time, until it's completely incorporated. Stir in the orange liqueur. Place a piece of plastic film or wax paper directly on the surface of the filling to prevent a skin from forming and refrigerate until it's quite firm, at least 2 hours. Then stir in the mascarpone and chill until you're ready to fill the cake.

3. For the cake, stir together the milk and honey in the bowl of an electric mixer until dissolved. Add the vanilla and yeast and set aside for a few minutes, until the yeast has proved itself worthy by bubbling encouragingly.

4. Add the egg, yolk, flour, salt, and zest. Stir everything together by hand until a very sticky dough forms. Cover the bowl with beeswax wrap or plastic film and let it rest for 15 minutes.

5. Using the electric mixer fitted with the paddle attachment, beat the dough on a lowish-medium speed for about 2 minutes, until things are looking pretty smooth. Add the butter a little bit at a time and continue beating for another 3 minutes, or until a sticky batter forms. Scrape down the sides of the bowl and beat a minute or

(continued)

two more. It won't look like anything much has happened. Scrape the so-called dough into a large buttered bowl and cover with beeswax wrap or plastic film. Set in a warm spot to rise until doubled in volume, about 1½ hours.

6. Lightly dust the still-sticky surface of the dough with flour and punch it down. Using a bowl scraper or a rubber spatula, work your way around the edge of the bowl, folding the dough into the center in 6 or 8 places, forming a messy ball. Cover the bowl and return to the warm spot to rise until doubled once more, about another hour.

7. Meanwhile, butter a 9 x 2-inch round cake pan.

8. Dust the surface of the dough with flour again and punch it down. Using both hands, tuck your fingers under two opposite sides of the dough and gently lift, gathering the dough underneath itself before placing it back down. Rotate the bowl and repeat two or three times, forming a neat ball. Gently pick up the ball and place it in the prepared pan, seam side down. Press the dough to the edges of the pan, stretching from the underside as you do pizza dough. Cover the pan with a large plate and set it aside to rise until the dough comes about two thirds of the way up the sides, about 1 hour.

9. About 30 minutes into this final rise, preheat the oven to 350°F (180°C) with a rack in the center position. Arrange the blood orange slices over the top of the dough, overlapping them this way and that. Sift confectioners' sugar over the orange slices.

10. Bake the cake until it's golden brown and the center reaches 200°F (93°C) on an instant-read thermometer, 40 to 45 minutes.

11. Transfer the cake to a wire rack. Let the cake cool in the pan for 5 minutes, then transfer to the rack to cool completely.

12. This simple glaze will shine things up. In a small saucepan, stir the blood orange juice and honey together and bring to a boil over medium heat. Cook for about 3 minutes, stirring frequently, until it's reduced by about half, then remove from the heat but keep warm.

13. Split the cooled cake in half horizontally with a long serrated knife (see page 247). Brush the bottom layer of the cake with some of the glaze and then spread the filling over it, leaving about a ¼-inch space around the edges. Top with the second cake layer and brush the glaze over the whole cake, but especially over the blood orange slices.

14. Chill the cake for about 30 minutes to help firm it up. Slice it with a serrated knife to serve.

STORAGE

The cake is really best the day you assemble it, but it can be covered and stored in the refrigerator for a few days, I suppose.

BOURBON PEACH KUGELHOPF

| MAKES 10 TO 12 SERVINGS | INTERMEDIATE | SPECIAL EQUIPMENT: 8-CUP KUGELHOPF OR BUNDT PAN, INSTANT-READ THERMOMETER |

Kugelhopf's classic golden crumb gets a Southern makeover in my version flecked with flavorful bourbon-soaked peaches. Sweetened with just a touch of honey, it's a perfect way to start the day. It's a perfect way to end it, too.

FOR THE PEACHES

roughly chopped dried peaches, in ½-inch pieces	1 cup	150 grams
bourbon	2 tablespoons	30 milliliters
sweet vermouth	2 tablespoons	30 milliliters
honey	2 tablespoons	40 grams

FOR THE SPONGE

whole milk, about 110°F (43°C)	⅔ cup	166 milliliters
honey	⅓ cup	107 grams
instant yeast (see page 10)	1½ teaspoons	4.5 grams
all-purpose flour	1 cup	142 grams

FOR THE DOUGH

large eggs	1 whole, plus 2 yolks	1 whole, plus 2 yolks
pure vanilla extract	1 tablespoon	15 milliliters
almond extract	1 teaspoon	5 milliliters
all-purpose flour, plus additional for dusting	1¾ cups	249 grams
coarse salt	1 teaspoon	3 grams
unsalted butter, softened, plus additional for the bowl and pan	½ cup (1 stick)	113 grams
sliced almonds	⅓ cup	35 grams

(continued)

FRUIT CAKE

honey	2 tablespoons	40 grams
bourbon	1 tablespoon	15 milliliters
sweet vermouth	1 tablespoon	15 milliliters

1. Toss the peaches with the bourbon, vermouth, and honey in a small bowl until generously coated, then let them sit for at least 1 hour while the booze does its thing.

2. Make the sponge: In the bowl of an electric mixer, stir together the milk, honey, and yeast until dissolved. Stir in the flour, forming a thin batter. Loosely cover the bowl with beeswax wrap or plastic film and set aside for about 15 minutes, until small bubbles form on the surface.

3. Make the dough: Add the egg, yolks, vanilla, and almond extract to the mixer bowl. Using the paddle attachment, mix on medium-low speed for 1 minute to combine. Add the flour and salt and continue mixing until the dough forms stringy webs as the mixer churns, 5 to 7 minutes. It's a sticky, wet dough that definitely won't clean the sides of the bowl, though you might get the feeling that it really wants to. Add the butter a little at a time and mix on medium speed for about 2 minutes, until the dough is smooth, shiny, and congregates around the base of the paddle (scrape down the sides of the bowl as needed). Add the peaches and any remaining liquid and mix on low speed until the pieces are evenly distributed.

4. Scrape the dough into a large buttered bowl. Cover with beeswax wrap or plastic film and set aside in a warm spot to rise until doubled, about 1½ hours.

5. Lightly dust the surface of the dough with flour and punch it down. Using a bowl scraper or rubber spatula, work your way around the edge of the bowl, folding the dough into the center in 6 or 8 places, forming a messy ball. Cover the bowl and let rise another hour or so, until doubled.

6. Busy yourself with brushing an 8-cup kugelhopf or Bundt pan with softened butter, then sprinkle the almonds around the bottom of the pan and shake gently to spread them around.

7. Lightly dust the dough with flour and punch down. Transfer to a well-floured work surface. Pat the dough into a rectangle about 8 x 12 inches, with a long side facing you. Fold the top third of the dough down toward the center of the rectangle and the bottom third up over the top. Using as much flour as you need, stretch and shape the dough into a log about 18 inches long. It will be soft, sticky, and a bit messy, a lot like ciabatta looks.

8. Carefully lift and lower the dough into the prepared pan, overlapping the ends. Cover the pan with a clean kitchen towel and let the dough rest until it's light, puffy, and full of air, about 1½ hours.

9. About 30 minutes before baking, preheat the oven to 350°F (180°C) with a rack in the lower-third position.

10. Bake the cake for 35 to 40 minutes, until it's golden brown and the center reaches 200°F (93°C) on an instant-read thermometer.

11. Remove the pan from the oven and flip the cake out onto a wire rack to let it cool slightly.

12. In a small saucepan, heat the honey, bourbon, and vermouth until just warm enough to dissolve, then brush over the cooling cake. Set aside to cool completely before serving.

STORAGE

The texture is best the day you bake it, but, when the cake is stored at room temperature in an airtight container, you'll find the flavor improves overnight. Lightly toast the slices to bring them back to life.

BIM'S YEAST CAKE

| MAKES 12 TO 14 SERVINGS | EASY |
| SPECIAL EQUIPMENT: 10-INCH TUBE PAN, INSTANT-READ THERMOMETER |

My grandmother probably never imagined using dried blueberries in this cake, but they serve an important function by imparting an intense blueberry flavor while cutting down on added moisture. The cake's impressive crown-like stature belies the fact that deep down in its soul it's a coffee cake, and that's nothing to be ashamed of.

FOR THE SPONGE

whole milk, warmed to about 95°F (35°C)	1 cup	250 milliliters
fresh yeast (see page 159)	1 ounce (2 tablespoons)	28 grams
all-purpose flour	1 cup	142 grams

FOR THE DOUGH

unsalted butter, softened	1 cup (2 sticks)	226 grams
granulated sugar	½ cup	106 grams
large eggs	2	2
all-purpose flour, plus additional for dusting	4 cups	568 grams
coarse salt	2 teaspoons	6 grams

FOR THE FILLING AND ASSEMBLY

Pan Goo (page 224), for greasing the pan		
granulated sugar	½ cup	106 grams
ground cinnamon	2 teaspoons	5 grams
fresh blueberries	¾ cup	105 grams
all-purpose flour, plus additional for dusting	1 tablespoon	9 grams
unsalted butter, melted, plus more for brushing	3 tablespoons	42 grams
dried blueberries	¾ cup	135 grams
finely chopped pecans, toasted (see page 18)	¼ cup	28 grams
large egg	1	1
coarse salt	1 pinch	1 pinch
pearl sugar, for sprinkling		

(continued)

confectioners' sugar	½ cup	57 grams
whole milk	1 to 2 tablespoons	15 to 30 milliliters

1. Make the sponge: In a medium bowl, whisk together the milk and yeast. Stir in the flour with a wooden spoon and set aside until the mixture is fully alive with billions of beautiful bubbles, about 20 minutes.

2. Make the dough: In the bowl of an electric mixer fitted with the paddle attachment, beat the butter and granulated sugar on medium speed until light and fluffy, 3 to 5 minutes. Scrape down the sides of the bowl with a rubber spatula. Add the eggs, one at a time, mixing well after each addition. Scrape down the bowl and add the flour and salt. Mix on low speed until a crumbly dough forms.

3. Scrape down the bowl once more and add the sponge. Switch to the dough hook attachment and mix on medium-low speed until the dough gathers around the hook and mostly cleans the sides of the bowl, 6 to 8 minutes.

4. Scrape the dough out onto a lightly floured surface and knead gently to form a ball. Return the dough to the mixer bowl, cover the bowl with beeswax wrap or plastic film, and let the dough rise in a warm place until doubled, about 1½ hours. Meanwhile, play a few rounds of gin rummy.

5. Generously brush a 10-inch tube pan with Pan Goo and set aside.

6. In a small bowl, whisk together the granulated sugar and cinnamon. In another small bowl, toss the fresh blueberries with the flour.

7. With floured hands, punch down the dough and transfer to a lightly floured surface. Dust the top of the dough with flour and roll it out into a 14 x 18-inch rectangle, with a long side facing you. Brush with about 2 tablespoons (28 grams) of the melted butter and sprinkle evenly with the cinnamon-sugar, fresh and dried blueberries, and pecans.

8. Starting on one of the long ends, roll the dough into a tight spiral, lifting and tugging the dough to capture all the nuts and berries. Gently place the dough in the prepared pan, seam side down, and overlap the ends. Brush with the remaining butter, including in the area between the overlapping ends of the dough. Cover the pan with beeswax wrap or plastic film and place in a warm spot to rise until doubled, about 1 hour.

9. At least 30 minutes before baking, preheat the oven to 350°F (180°C) with a rack in the lower-third position.

10. Lightly beat together the egg and salt. When the dough has risen, brush the top of the cake with the beaten egg and sprinkle liberally with pearl sugar. Cut slits on the bias about 1 inch deep using kitchen shears.

11. Bake until the cake is deep golden brown and firm to the touch and an instant-read thermometer registers 200°F (93°C), 60 to 70 minutes.

12. Transfer the pan to a wire rack. Let the cake rest in the pan for 15 minutes, then carefully flip it out and invert it again onto the rack to cool completely.

13. Make the glaze: In a small bowl, whisk together the confectioners' sugar with about 1 tablespoon of milk. Continue adding milk by the teaspoonful until it forms a glaze that coats the back of a spoon. Drizzle over the cake in diagonal swaths. Slice with a serrated knife to serve.

STORAGE

This cake is best the day it's baked, but it can be stored in an airtight container at room temperature for up to 2 days.

FRESH YEAST

I've called for fresh yeast rather than instant in this recipe because that is what my grandmother used. Fresh yeast was the only type available when she learned her craft in the first half of the twentieth century. Even after active dry yeast was invented during World War II, fresh yeast has maintained a following among the nostalgic, who appreciate its sweet aroma and soft crumbles. These days, the market is dominated by active dry and instant yeast (which didn't arrive on the scene until the 1980s). Fresh yeast can be found in the refrigerated section of a grocery store, but if it's unavailable, see the chart on page 11 for substitutions.

CINNAMON RAISIN BUNS

| MAKES 8 SERVINGS | EASY |
| SPECIAL EQUIPMENT: BENCH SCRAPER, INSTANT-READ THERMOMETER |

Okay, I'll confess. It's hard to call this a cake. But it's a blurry line when there's a swirl of cinnamon sugar and plump, juicy raisins hiding around every twist and turn. Since you made it yourself, you can eat this for breakfast with no hesitation. You're welcome.

FOR THE DOUGH

granulated sugar	2 tablespoons	27 grams
instant yeast (see page 10)	1 teaspoon	3 grams
whole milk, warmed to about 110°F (43°C)	½ cup	125 milliliters
large eggs	1 whole, plus 1 yolk	1 whole, plus 1 yolk
pure vanilla extract	1 teaspoon	5 milliliters
finely grated orange zest (from 1 orange)	1 teaspoon	2 grams
all-purpose flour, plus additional for dusting	2 cups	284 grams
coarse salt	1 teaspoon	3 grams
unsalted butter, very soft, plus additional for greasing the pan	4 tablespoons (½ stick)	57 grams

FOR THE FILLING

golden raisins, preferably hunza	½ cup	80 grams
boiling water	¼ cup	62 milliliters
unsalted butter, softened	4 tablespoons (½ stick)	57 grams
ground cinnamon	2 teaspoons	5 grams
firmly packed light brown sugar	¼ cup	53 grams
coarsely crumbled walnuts	⅓ cup	34 grams

FOR THE GLAZE

whole milk	1 to 2 tablespoons	15 to 30 milliliters
confectioners' sugar	½ cup	56 grams

(continued)

1. In a medium bowl, stir the granulated sugar and yeast into the warm milk and let stand for about 5 minutes, until bubbles form on the surface. Add the egg, yolk, vanilla, and orange zest, whisking until well combined. Stir in the flour and salt with a wooden spoon until a thick, shaggy dough forms. Cover the bowl with beeswax wrap or plastic film and let the dough rest for 15 minutes while the flour hydrates.

2. Butter a large bowl. Turn the dough out onto a lightly floured surface and knead. Give yourself over to the dough! Use both hands and a bench scraper to help lift it off the work surface. Don't even think about answering the phone. After about 5 minutes, when the dough is significantly less sticky, begin to work in the butter, a little bit at a time. It will seem almost impossible at first; the dough will become slick and difficult to handle. Keep at it. When all the butter has been incorporated as best it can be, the dough will be sticky, supple, soft, and stretchy. Use quick, nimble movements to shape the dough roughly into a ball and slap it into the center of the buttered bowl. Cover the bowl again and let it rise until doubled, about 1½ hours.

3. Flip the dough back onto a lightly floured surface. It will be remarkably easier to handle. Gently press the dough into an 8-inch square, releasing some of the larger bubbles. Fold the top half of the dough down to meet the bottom and then the left half over to meet the right. Return the dough to the buttered bowl, cover once more, and let rise until doubled, this time for about 1 hour.

4. Meanwhile, stir the raisins into the boiling water and let them sit for at least 30 minutes, until the liquid has been mostly absorbed. Brush a 9 x 2-inch round cake pan with butter.

5. In a medium bowl, stir together the butter, cinnamon, and light brown sugar until it forms a smooth paste.

6. Back on the lightly floured surface, roll the dough into a square 12 inches across. Use a small offset spatula to spread the butter and brown sugar mixture across the dough, leaving about a ½-inch border. Scatter the raisins and walnuts evenly on top. Roll the dough firmly into a spiraled log, trapping all the goodies inside. Use a sharp serrated knife to cut the log into 8 equal pieces and arrange them (cut sides up) in the prepared pan, 7 around the perimeter and 1 in the center. Invert a large bowl and place it over the pan. Set it aside until the buns are approximately doubled in size, about 45 minutes.

7. About 30 minutes before baking, preheat the oven to 350°F (180°C) with a rack in the center position.

8. Bake the buns until they're puffy and golden brown and an instant-read thermometer inserted into the center reads 200°F (93°C), 35 to 40 minutes.

9. Set aside to cool slightly while you make the glaze. Stir the milk into the confectioners' sugar a little at a time, until the mixture is smooth and coats the back of a spoon. Drizzle the glaze over the warm buns and use an offset spatula to serve straight out of the pan.

BREAKFAST BUDDIES

If you want these buns ready early in the morning, you can cover the dough and pop it in the refrigerator after completing the folds in step 3, rather than letting it rise for 1 hour. Soak the raisins overnight, too, then pick up in the morning at step 4, keeping in mind that it may take closer to 90 minutes for the shaped buns to rise.

CONCORD GRAPE FOCACCIA

| DAIRY-FREE | MAKES 10 TO 12 SERVINGS | EASY | OVERNIGHT |
| SPECIAL EQUIPMENT: INSTANT-READ THERMOMETER |

This is the focaccia of my childhood memories, light and fluffy, salty and sweet, and probably completely inauthentic. The smattering of Concord grapes are little flavor bombs set to go off at any moment. I like crunching down on their seeds, but if you prefer a seedless variety of grape you have my blessing. It's not exactly dessert, but this is my type of midnight snack.

FOR THE DOUGH

olive oil, plus additional for the pan	¼ cup	62 milliliters
instant yeast (see page 10)	1 teaspoon	3 grams
all-purpose flour	2 cups	284 grams
bread flour	1½ cups	180 grams
granulated sugar	¼ cup	53 grams
coarse salt	1 tablespoon	9 grams

FOR THE BRINE AND ASSEMBLY

warm water	2 tablespoons	30 milliliters
olive oil	2 tablespoons	30 milliliters
coarse salt	1 teaspoon	3 grams
grapes, preferably Concord	1 heaping cup	165 grams
sanding sugar, for sprinkling		

1. Mix the dough while you're cleaning up from dinner the evening before baking. Combine 1¾ cups water, the oil, and yeast in a measuring cup and stir until the yeast dissolves. In a large bowl, whisk together both flours, the granulated sugar, and salt. Stir the wet ingredients into the dry with a wooden spoon until all the flour has been moistened, then cover the bowl with beeswax wrap or plastic film and refrigerate for at least 12 hours or up to 2 days.

2. In the morning, take the bowl out of the fridge and place it in a warm spot for about 1 hour to take the chill off. Coat a 9 x 13-inch glass baking dish with olive oil and line the bottom and two long sides with a sheet of parchment paper, leaving about 2 inches overhanging the sides. Oil the parchment paper, too.

3. Scrape the dough into the baking dish and, with oiled fingers, dimple the dough, pressing outward from the center until it reaches all the

(continued)

corners. Let the dough rise in the warm spot until it fills the baking dish halfway, about 2 hours.

4. About 30 minutes before baking, preheat the oven to 425°F (220°C) with a rack in the center position.

5. In a small bowl, make the brine by whisking together the water, oil, and salt. Scatter the grapes across the dough and then drizzle the brine over the surface, letting it soak in for a minute or so before sprinkling with sanding sugar.

6. Bake the focaccia for about 30 minutes, until it's deep golden brown and firm to the touch and an instant-read thermometer inserted into the center reads 200°F (93°C).

7. Transfer the baking dish to a wire rack. Run a sharp knife along the short sides of the baking dish, then, using the overhanging parchment paper as handles, lift out the focaccia. Slide it off the parchment onto the rack to cool as long as you can bear. I wouldn't recommend waiting too long.

STORAGE

This focaccia is best served the day it's baked but can be kept reasonably well in an airtight container for up to 2 days.

STARTING OUT

You'll get a lot of focaccia out of this recipe with minimal effort, which makes it a perfect entrée to the bread-baking fold. You could also make it a savory situation by eliminating the sugar and replacing the grapes with just about anything you can imagine.

NOCTURNE (THINGS THAT WORRY ME)

People, will you stop pretending

Life on this earth isn't ending?

Have you even stopped to think

Bananas soon could go extinct?

Coastal lands are fast eroding

Deserts are forever growing

Garbage piles up on the beach

Do I dare to eat a peach?

Last night I could hardly sleep

Worried I'd miscounted sheep

I could slip on sidewalk tiles

Dodging cyclists riding wild

Even eating nonorganic

Strawberries could make me panic

I fear too that I'll grow fatter

Eating all of this cake batter

But in truth what could it matter?

PANETTONE TROPICALE

| MAKES ONE 6½-INCH ROUND LOAF | INTERMEDIATE | MULTIDAY | SPECIAL
EQUIPMENT: 6½ x 4-INCH PAPER PANETTONE MOLD, INSTANT-READ THERMOMETER |

Let me say at the outset that although this recipe takes five days (I know), most of that time asks little of you. It is possible to rush it, and I've tried, but rushing is not my style. The flavors that develop over days of slow fermentation are not something to shortchange yourself of. This is a beast of a cake, and lovingly lavishing attention upon it is what makes it so glorious.

Besides, the holidays come but once a year. Laden with butter, eggs, and candied fruit, this panettone is rich, just sweet enough, and unexpectedly light in texture. It's no surprise that this cake, with roots in ancient Rome, has stood the test of time.

Here's how I would go about this multiday project:

Day One, evening: Make the biga.
Day Two: Make the bed.
Day Three, evening: Make the starter dough.
Day Four, midday: Mix the final dough and let the dough rise at room temperature.
Day Four, evening: Shape the dough and transfer to the refrigerator to rise overnight.
Day Five, morning: Let the dough rise at room temperature.
Day Five, late afternoon: Bake the panettone.

FOR THE BIGA

bread flour	½ cup	60 grams
instant yeast (see page 10)	¼ teaspoon	0.8 gram
water, warmed to about 110°F (43°C)	⅓ cup	83 milliliters

FOR THE STARTER DOUGH

whole milk, warmed to about 110°F (43°C)	¼ cup	62 milliliters
instant yeast (see page 10)	1¼ teaspoons	3.8 grams
large eggs	2 whole, plus 2 yolks	2 whole, plus 2 yolks
Lyle's Golden Syrup or honey	2 tablespoons	44 grams
pure vanilla extract	1 tablespoon	15 milliliters
bread flour	½ cup	60 grams

(continued)

granulated sugar	⅓ cup	71 grams
instant yeast (see page 10)	1 tablespoon	9 grams
finely grated orange zest (from 1 orange)	1 teaspoon	2 grams
all-purpose flour, plus additional for dusting	2 cups	284 grams
coarse salt	2 teaspoons	6 grams
unsalted butter, softened, plus additional for greasing the bowl	½ cup (1 stick)	113 grams
coarsely chopped candied papaya	½ cup	85 grams
coarsely chopped candied mango	½ cup	85 grams
finely chopped candied citron	½ cup	95 grams
finely chopped orange Candied Citrus Peel (page 236)	½ cup	90 grams

large egg white, lightly beaten	1	1

FRUIT CAKE

1. On an evening early in the week, when you're getting into the spirit of things, make the biga, which is an Italian term for *preferment,* a method of adding structure and flavor to yeasted doughs. Stir together the bread flour, yeast, and water in a small bowl, mixing gently with a rubber spatula until you get a sticky, wet batter. Cover the bowl with beeswax wrap or plastic film and let it sit at room temperature for about 2 hours, until it's nearly tripled in volume. Then stir vigorously, cover again, and refrigerate for 2 to 3 days.

2. This next step is just about as mindless as the first. Scrape the biga into a large bowl. In a measuring cup, whisk the milk, yeast, eggs, yolks, golden syrup, and vanilla, then pour over the biga, stirring to combine. Don't worry about dissolving it completely. Stir in the bread flour until a wet, dare I say *gluey,* batter forms. Cover the bowl with a plate and let it rise for 1 hour at room temperature, then refrigerate for at least 12 hours or up to 1 day.

3. I know you're waiting for things to get serious, but the truth is no part of this recipe is all that complicated. When you're ready to make the final dough, scrape the starter dough into the bowl of an electric mixer. Add the sugar, yeast, orange zest, and all-purpose flour. Stir briefly with a rubber spatula until a shaggy dough forms, then cover the bowl with beeswax wrap or plastic film and let it rest for 15 minutes so the flour can fully hydrate.

4. Add the salt to the bowl. Using the electric mixer fitted with the paddle attachment, mix the dough on low speed for about 2 minutes, until a wet, stringy, and decidedly not smooth dough forms. Begin adding the butter, about 1 tablespoon at a time, waiting until each addition is completely incorporated before adding the next.

168

(continued)

Continue mixing on low speed until the dough becomes so smooth and shiny you can't resist touching it—and when you do it's luxuriously soft, supple, and just barely tacky—10 to 15 minutes. The dough will clean the sides of the mixer bowl but may not completely clean the bottom. (If you feel like it needs a bit of help coming together, or are using a smaller-size mixer, scrape down the sides of the bowl and the paddle a few times throughout mixing.)

5. Turn the dough out onto a lightly floured surface and gently pat into a disc about 10 inches across. Load up the center of the circle with the candied fruit and gather the edges of the dough as you would a beggar's purse, locking the fruit inside. Gently knead the dough into a ball. Place in a large buttered bowl, cover with beeswax wrap or plastic film, and let it rise until doubled in volume, about 2 hours.

6. Flip the dough out onto a lightly floured surface and gently press into a square about 10 inches across. Fold the top half of the square down to meet the bottom and then the left half over to meet the right. Flatten the dough into a square once more. This time the dough will be stiffer and offer more resistance; you may only be able to stretch it to about 8 inches. Repeat the folds as you've just done them. Tuck the edges of the dough under and gently shape into a ball.

7. Return the dough to the buttered bowl, cover, and let rise until doubled, about 1 hour.

8. Flip the dough once more onto a lightly floured surface. Repeat step 6.

9. Slip the dough (with the seams on the bottom) into a 6½ x 4-inch paper panettone mold. Cover the mold with beeswax wrap or plastic film and refrigerate overnight, 8 to 12 hours.

10. In the morning, pull the panettone out of the refrigerator and place in a warm, draft-free spot. Let the dough rise until the edges of the ball are about ½ inch below the top of the paper mold. When gently pressed, the dough will feel firm, tight, and springy like a foam pillow. This may take 6 hours; it's important not to rush it.

11. About 30 minutes before baking, preheat the oven to 350°F (180°C) with a rack in the lower-third position.

12. Brush the surface of the dough with the lightly beaten egg white. Place the panettone on a baking sheet and transfer to the oven.

13. Bake the panettone for 20 minutes, then reduce the temperature to 300°F (150°C). Continue baking until the cake is golden brown and firm to the touch and an instant-read thermometer inserted into the center reads 185°F (85°C), about 40 minutes longer, tenting with foil if the top darkens too quickly.

14. Remove the baking sheet from the oven. Let the cake cool completely, then use a sharp, serrated knife to cut right through the paper mold to serve tall slender slices.

STORAGE

Panettones keep remarkably well in an airtight container at room temperature. They also make great toast.

ROSCA DE REYES

| MAKES 12 TO 14 SERVINGS | INTERMEDIATE | OVERNIGHT |
| SPECIAL EQUIPMENT: INSTANT-READ THERMOMETER |

Rosca de Reyes loosely translates to "Kings' Cake," and indeed the two pastries have a lot in common. I was introduced to roscas the first time Eddie brought me to Mexico, where it's served on Three Kings' Day rather than Mardi Gras. There, the cake is loaded with candied citrus and finished with the crispy, crackly topping typical of *concha*, the sweet little rolls that fill the shelves of neighborhood *panaderías*. Only one bite has an almond or a figurine inside—as tradition has it, whoever finds it is on the hook for making tamales in early February on Día de la Candelaria.

FOR THE DOUGH

instant yeast (see page 10)	4½ teaspoons (two ¼-ounce envelopes)	14 grams
whole milk, warmed to about 110°F (43°C)	½ cup	125 milliliters
large eggs	1 whole, plus 1 yolk	1 whole, plus 1 yolk
granulated sugar	⅓ cup	71 grams
pure vanilla extract	1 teaspoon	5 milliliters
all-purpose flour, plus additional for dusting	1¼ cups	178 grams
bread flour	1¼ cups	150 grams
coarse salt	1½ teaspoons	4.5 grams
unsalted butter, softened, plus additional for greasing the bowl	6 tablespoons (¾ stick)	85 grams
finely diced orange Candied Citrus Peel (page 236)	¼ cup	45 grams

(continued)

all-purpose flour	¼ cup	36 grams
granulated sugar	¼ cup	53 grams
pure vanilla extract	½ teaspoon	2.5 milliliters
unsalted butter, softened	4 tablespoons (½ stick)	57 grams
whole almond	1	1
large egg	1	1
coarse salt	1 pinch	1 pinch
mixed Candied Citrus Peel (page 236 and see note opposite), thinly sliced into strips about 2 inches long	⅓ cup	60 grams
sanding sugar, for sprinkling		

1. In a small bowl, stir the yeast into the warm milk with a fork or a small whisk. Let stand until the surface is foamy, about 5 minutes. Meanwhile, in the bowl of an electric mixer, whisk the egg, yolk, granulated sugar, and vanilla. Add the milk mixture and whisk to combine, then add the flours. Stir together with a wooden spoon until a very shaggy dough forms, then cover the bowl with beeswax wrap or plastic film and let rest for 10 minutes to allow the flour to hydrate.

2. Add the salt to the bowl. Using the electric mixer fitted with the dough hook attachment, mix the dough on low speed until it forms a stiff ball, about 3 minutes.

3. Begin adding the butter, about 1 tablespoon at a time. Aim for the center of the bowl and wait until each addition of butter has been almost completely incorporated before adding the next. It should take about 6 more minutes to add it all, bit by bit. It may seem at times like the dough is vehemently opposed to the idea of the butter. When that happens, stop the machine and scrape the dough off the hook. Then keep going. When all the butter has been added, continue kneading

until the dough is smooth and elastic and begins to clean the sides of the bowl, about 5 minutes longer. It may seem like nothing is happening at first, but in time the dough will come together with a satisfying snap. Mix in the candied orange peel until it's evenly dispersed.

4. Butter a large bowl. With buttered hands, use quick, nimble movements to shape the dough into a ball, place it in the bowl, and cover again. Set the bowl in a warm spot and let it rise undisturbed until doubled, about 1½ hours. Flip the dough out onto a lightly floured work surface and press into a square about 12 inches across. Fold the top half down to meet the bottom and then the left half over to meet the right. Press the dough out into a square once more. It will be stiffer and more difficult to shape; you may only be able to stretch it to about 9 inches. Fold in quarters again and then tuck the edges under to form a ball. Return the dough to the bowl (with the seams on the bottom), cover, and refrigerate for at least 4 hours, ideally overnight.

5. Meanwhile, make the topping: In a small bowl, stir together the all-purpose flour, granulated

sugar, and vanilla. Using your fingers, work the butter into the flour mixture until it forms a paste. Cover and refrigerate until ready to use.

6. Line a 13 x 18-inch rimmed baking sheet with a silicone baking mat or parchment paper.

7. Turn the dough out onto a clean work surface and flatten into a disc. Use your thumbs to punch a hole in the center of the dough. Gently stretch the dough into a ring, squeezing it between your fists until it's about 1½ inches thick. Arrange the ring into an oval about 10 inches long and 8 inches wide on the prepared baking sheet. Carefully tuck the almond into the ring from the underside. Lightly cover the cake with a clean kitchen towel and set aside until the dough is light, puffy, and full of air but does not feel fragile. This could take 2 to 4 hours, depending on how warm your kitchen is.

8. At least 30 minutes before baking, preheat the oven to 350°F (180°C) with a rack in the center position.

9. Lightly beat the egg and salt until well combined, then use it to brush the surface of the cake.

10. Pinch off pieces of the refrigerated topping about the size of grapes and flatten between your fingers into ovals about 3 inches long. Arrange the topping over the cake in a decorative pattern, leaving space for the candied citrus. Place strips of candied citrus in between and on top of the topping, then sprinkle generously with sanding sugar.

11. Bake the rosca until golden brown and an instant-read thermometer reads 185°F (85°C), about 22 minutes.

12. Remove the baking sheet from the oven, and allow the rosca to cool completely on the pan.

STORAGE

The cake is best eaten the day it's baked but can be kept in an airtight container at room temperature for up to 3 days.

FRESHLY CANDIED CITRUS

I prefer to use freshly candied citrus that has been stored in its syrup for recipes like this, where some of the fruit is fully exposed to the heat of the oven. Squeeze off as much liquid as you can before using; the small amount of syrup that clings to the peel will help to keep it tender throughout baking. If you don't have fresh on hand, look for the juiciest candied citrus you can find.

STOLLEN

Panettone's shorter, German nephew, stollen (pronounced "shtollen") contains so much dried fruit and nuts you may wonder if the dough will ever come together. Have faith; it will. There are many styles of stollen, but my favorite has a ribbon of marzipan coursing through the center. Untraditional, maybe. Delicious, yes.

Letting the dough rest in the refrigerator overnight makes it much easier to shape and the stollen even more flavorful.

FOR THE FRUIT MIXTURE

golden raisins, preferably hunza	½ cup	80 grams
finely chopped dried apricots	½ cup	90 grams
dried currants	¼ cup	35 grams
dark rum	⅓ cup	83 milliliters

FOR THE DOUGH

instant yeast (see page 10)	2¼ teaspoons (one ¼-ounce envelope)	7 grams
whole milk, warmed to about 110°F (43°C)	½ cup	125 milliliters
large eggs	1 whole, plus 1 yolk	1 whole, plus 1 yolk
granulated sugar	¼ cup	53 grams
pure vanilla extract	2 teaspoons	10 milliliters
finely grated lemon zest (from 1 lemon)	1 teaspoon	2 grams
all-purpose flour, plus additional for dusting	2¼ cups	320 grams
freshly ground cardamom (see page 11)	½ teaspoon	1 gram
ground cinnamon	½ teaspoon	1.3 grams
coarse salt	1 teaspoon	3 grams
unsalted butter, softened, plus additional for greasing the bowl	4 tablespoons (½ stick)	57 grams
finely chopped almonds	¼ cup	56 grams
finely chopped orange Candied Citrus Peel (page 236)	⅓ cup	60 grams
marzipan (not almond paste)	about ⅓ cup (3.5 ounces)	about 100 grams

(continued)   **177**

unsalted butter, melted	3 tablespoons	42 grams
confectioners' sugar, for dusting		

1. In a small bowl, combine all the ingredients for the fruit mixture. Cover and set aside at room temperature for at least 2 hours or overnight.

2. In another small bowl, sprinkle the yeast over the warm milk and stir to combine. Let stand for about 5 minutes, until the yeast softens.

3. Meanwhile, in the bowl of an electric mixer, whisk together the egg, yolk, granulated sugar, vanilla, and lemon zest. Whisk the milk mixture into the egg mixture and add the flour, cardamom, and cinnamon. Use a rubber spatula or a wooden spoon to stir until a dry, shaggy dough forms. Cover the bowl with beeswax wrap or plastic film and set aside for 15 minutes while the flour hydrates.

4. Add the salt to the bowl. Using the electric mixer fitted with the dough hook attachment, knead the dough on low speed until a strong, stiff dough forms, about 3 minutes. Add the butter about 1 tablespoon at a time, waiting until each addition has been incorporated before adding the next. Continue kneading on low speed until the dough cleans the sides of the bowl and forms a soft, smooth ball that is just barely tacky to the touch, about 6 minutes.

5. Add the soaked fruit, almonds, and candied orange peel. Don't be alarmed; it will look like there is more fruit and nuts than dough. Continue kneading on low speed for about 2 minutes, until evenly distributed. The dough may no longer clean the bowl, but it will be soft and strong, even though it looks a bit stringy.

6. Scrape the dough into a buttered bowl and, with buttered hands, roughly shape into a ball. It will be heavy with fruit. Cover the bowl with beeswax wrap or plastic film and let rise in a warm spot until doubled in volume, about 1½ hours.

7. Flip the dough out onto a floured surface. Pat into a square about 12 inches across. Fold the top half down to meet the bottom and the left half over to meet the right. Press into a square once more; it will be stiffer now and more difficult to stretch, and you may get it to only 10 inches across. Fold the dough in quarters again, then tuck the edges under to form a ball.

8. Return to the buttered bowl (with the seams on the bottom), cover, and refrigerate overnight.

9. In the morning, flip the dough out onto a lightly floured surface. Use a bench scraper or a knife to cut the dough in half.

10. Line a 13 x 18-inch rimmed baking sheet with a silicone baking mat or a piece of parchment paper.

11. Begin the shaping process, working with one piece of dough at a time: Place one piece on a floured surface with the cut edge face down. Press firmly with the palm of your hand, flattening the dough into an oval that's about 9 inches wide and 6 inches across. Flip the dough over so the raggedy seams are on the top and continue gently shaping until it resembles (I'm told) a deflated football.

12. Divide the marzipan in half. Using the heels of your hands, roll one piece of marzipan into a log about 6 inches long and place it along the 9-inch equator of the dough, centered with extra dough on both sides. Lightly brush the entire surface of the dough with water. Fold the bottom edge of dough over the marzipan, pressing firmly with the side of your hand to trap the marzipan inside. Fold the top edge down to almost—but not quite—meet the side

of the dough closest to you, pressing firmly to seal. Pinch the pointy ends of the dough to make sure the marzipan doesn't try to make a run for it. Gently lift the shaped stollen and set on the baking sheet, angling it about 45 degrees so that you can fit both loaves on the same pan.

13. Repeat the shaping process with the second piece of dough and arrange it on the baking sheet, about 2 inches from the first. Lightly cover both loaves with beeswax wrap or plastic film and place in a warm spot to rise until the loaves are light and full of air and spring back slowly when gently pressed, about 2 hours.

14. About 30 minutes before baking, preheat the oven to 375°F (190°C) with a rack in the center position. Bake the loaves until golden brown and firm to the touch and an instant-read thermometer inserted into the center reads 185°F (85°C), about 28 minutes.

15. Transfer the baking sheet to a wire rack. Let the loaves cool on the pan for about 5 minutes, then transfer to the rack. While the loaves are still warm, brush the entire surface of each with melted butter and dust liberally with confectioners' sugar, rubbing it in to saturate it.

16. Set aside to cool completely, then store in an airtight container overnight to let the flavors mature before serving, if you can wait that long. Dust with additional confectioners' sugar just before serving if you desire a fresh look.

STORAGE

Because of its generous coating of butter and sugar, stollen keeps remarkably well. Store in an airtight container at room temperature for up to 1 week, or freeze, well wrapped, for up to 3 months.

NECTARINE KUCHEN

In German, *Kuchen* can describe virtually any cake, but here in the States the name calls to mind a soft, yeast-risen, fruit-topped number often named after Midwestern grannies. This cake is only as sweet as the fruit you top it with, so make sure to use something ripe-as-can-be. If nectarines aren't your thing, feel free to swap in any stone fruit of your choosing.

FOR THE CAKE

whole milk, warmed to about 110°F (43°C)	½ cup	125 milliliters
instant yeast (see page 10)	1 teaspoon	3 grams
all-purpose flour	1½ cups	213 grams
granulated sugar	6 tablespoons	80 grams
coarse salt	1 teaspoon	3 grams
large eggs	1 whole, plus 1 yolk	1 whole, plus 1 yolk
pure vanilla extract	1 teaspoon	5 milliliters
finely grated lemon zest (from 1 lemon)	1 teaspoon	2 grams
unsalted butter, softened, plus additional for greasing the bowl and pan	6 tablespoons (¾ stick)	85 grams

FOR ASSEMBLY

firm-ripe nectarines, pitted and cut into ½-inch slices	2 (about 12 ounces total)	340 grams
bourbon	2 tablespoons	30 milliliters
firmly packed dark brown sugar	2 tablespoons	27 grams
unsalted butter, cold and cut into small pieces	1 tablespoon	14 grams
pearl sugar, for sprinkling		

(continued)

1. Combine the milk and yeast in a small bowl and stir until the yeast dissolves. Set aside for about 5 minutes, until the yeast is foamy and champing at the bit.

2. In the bowl of an electric mixer fitted with the paddle attachment, place the flour, granulated sugar, and salt. With the mixer running on low speed, add the milk mixture, egg, yolk, vanilla, and lemon zest. Continue to mix until all the ingredients have been moistened, then increase the speed to medium and beat for about 5 minutes, until the dough is stringy and elastic. Scrape down the sides of the bowl and scrape off the paddle, then begin adding the butter a little at a time while mixing on medium speed. Keep beating until the butter is completely incorporated, about 5 minutes. Scrape what can reasonably only be described as a batter into a buttered bowl, cover with beeswax wrap or plastic film, and let rise until doubled, about 1 hour.

3. Preheat the oven to 375°F (190°C) with a rack in the center position. Brush a 9-inch glass or ceramic pie plate with butter.

4. Scrape the dough into the center of the dish and spread (it's more of a smear) it up the sides. Invert a large bowl over the pie plate and set aside to rise until light and full of air, about 45 minutes.

5. In the meantime, combine the nectarines, bourbon, and dark brown sugar in a medium bowl and toss to combine.

6. Arrange the nectarine slices on top of the dough, nestling them gently into place. Dot with the butter and sprinkle with pearl sugar.

7. Bake the cake until it's firm to the touch and an instant-read thermometer inserted into the center reads 185°F (85°C), about 32 minutes.

8. Remove the baking dish from the oven and allow the cake to cool in the plate. Serve warm or at room temperature.

STORAGE

The cake is best the day it's baked but can be stored in an airtight container at room temperature for up to 1 day.

CHOCOLATE ORANGE BABKA

| MAKES ABOUT 8 SERVINGS | ADVANCED | OVERNIGHT |

The number of babkas I made while working on this recipe is second only to the number of babkas I ate. It was worth the struggle; this one is my idea of perfect. It's soft and sticky, but not too sticky. Sweet, but not too sweet, and loaded with chocolate without being difficult to handle. I've called for a sweeter percentage of chocolate to balance the bitterness of the marmalade. For those who simply can't stand the orange stuff, feel free to swap in another flavor of jam at your discretion.

    Refrigerating the dough overnight makes the dough easier to shape and the babka more flavorful.

FOR THE DOUGH

whole milk, warmed to about 110°F (43°C)	½ cup	125 milliliters
instant yeast (see page 10)	4½ teaspoons (two ¼-ounce envelopes)	14 grams
large eggs	1 whole, plus 1 yolk	1 whole, plus 1 yolk
granulated sugar	⅓ cup	71 grams
pure vanilla extract	2 teaspoons	10 milliliters
finely grated orange zest (from 1 orange)	1 teaspoon	2 grams
all-purpose flour, plus additional for dusting	2½ cups	355 grams
freshly ground cardamom (see page 11)	1 teaspoon	2 grams
coarse salt	1 teaspoon	3 grams
unsalted butter, softened, plus additional for greasing the bowl	4 tablespoons (½ stick)	57 grams

FOR THE FILLING

best-quality dark chocolate, preferably around 55% cacao, finely chopped	1¾ ounces	50 grams
unsalted butter	3 tablespoons	42 grams
confectioners' sugar	3 tablespoons	21 grams
unsweetened cocoa powder, preferably Dutch-processed	2 tablespoons	10 grams
coarse salt	1 pinch	1 pinch
orange marmalade	3 tablespoons	45 grams

(continued) **183**

| orange marmalade | ½ cup | 120 grams |
| orange liqueur, such as Triple Sec | 2 tablespoons | 30 milliliters |

1. In a small bowl, combine the milk and yeast and let stand until the yeast softens, about 5 minutes.

2. In the bowl of an electric mixer, whisk together the egg, yolk, granulated sugar, vanilla, and orange zest. Whisk the milk and yeast into the egg mixture, then stir in the flour and cardamom until a dry, shaggy dough forms. Cover the bowl with beeswax wrap or plastic film and let the dough sit for 15 minutes to hydrate.

3. Add the salt to the bowl. Using the electric mixer fitted with the dough hook attachment, knead the dough on low speed for about 3 minutes, until it is sticky, smooth, and cleans the sides of the bowl. Begin adding the butter, about 1 tablespoon at a time, waiting until each piece has been incorporated before adding the next. Continue kneading on low speed, stopping to scrape down the sides of the bowl occasionally, until the dough is soft and elastic, just a bit tacky to the touch, and once again cleans the sides (but probably not the bottom) of the bowl, 6 to 8 minutes.

4. Using a bowl scraper or a rubber spatula, scrape the dough into a buttered bowl and, with buttered hands and quick movements, shape into a tight ball. Cover the bowl with beeswax wrap or plastic film and set in a warm spot to rise until doubled in volume, about 1½ hours.

5. Flip the dough out of the bowl onto a floured surface and press into a square about 10 inches across. Fold the top half down to meet the bottom and the left half over to meet the right. Press the dough out into a square once more; it will be stiffer now and may stretch to only about 8 or 9 inches. Fold in quarters again. Tuck the edges of the dough under and shape into a ball.

6. Return the dough to the buttered bowl (with the seams on the bottom), cover, and refrigerate for 8 to 12 hours. Sleep well.

7. In the morning, make the babka filling before you take the dough out of the refrigerator. Combine the chocolate and butter in a small heatproof bowl. Set over a pan of gently simmering water and heat, stirring occasionally, until melted, about 2 minutes. Remove from the heat and stir in the confectioners' sugar, cocoa powder, and salt. Set aside to cool slightly.

8. Brush a standard 8½ x 4½-inch loaf pan with butter and line the bottom and two long sides with a sheet of parchment paper, leaving about 2 inches overhanging the sides.

9. Flip the dough out of the bowl onto a well-floured surface. Lightly dust the top of the dough with flour and roll into a rectangle that's about 12 x 14 inches, with a short side facing you. Use a small offset spatula to spread the chocolate filling over the dough, leaving about a ½-inch border around the edges. Drop tablespoons of marmalade on top of the chocolate filling and spread to form a thin, even layer. Beginning at the side closest to you, roll the dough around the filling, forming a tightly spiraled log. Transfer the dough to a rimmed baking sheet and freeze for about 15 minutes, until firm enough to slice.

10. Return the log to the work surface with a short end facing you. Use a sharp knife to slice the log in half lengthwise and open like a book, exposing all the layers of dough and filling. Carefully lift the left strand of dough and cross

(continued)

it over the right, forming an X in the center. Starting in the center and working toward the ends, twist the two strands over and under each other, always keeping the cut sides face up, forming a spiral known as a Russian braid.

11. Gingerly scoop the shaped loaf off the work surface and lower it into the prepared pan, tucking the ends of the dough under as you do. Set the pan in a warm spot to rise until the dough is light and full of air and crests about 1 inch above the top of the pan, about 1½ hours.

12. At least 30 minutes before baking, preheat the oven to 325°F (170°C) with a rack in the center position. When the dough is ready to bake, set the loaf pan on a rimmed baking sheet to catch any drips.

13. Bake the babka until it's golden brown and firm to the touch and an instant-read thermometer inserted into the center reads 185°F (85°C), about 1 hour, tenting with foil if the top darkens too quickly.

14. Remove the pan from the oven and make the syrup: In a small saucepan, whisk the marmalade, orange liqueur, and 2 tablespoons water. Stir over medium heat until the mixture is loose enough to pour easily, about 45 seconds. Strain the syrup through a coarse-mesh sieve and slowly pour over the cooling babka, letting it work its way down through all the crevasses.

15. Allow the babka to cool completely in the loaf pan, then use the overhanging parchment paper as handles to lift it out.

STORAGE

The babka will keep for a few days in an airtight container at room temperature.

SOAKED

If you've never been in love with a traditional fruitcake, I think you've made an error in judgment. Worse, if you've never even tried one. You'll find some here, and some new inventions, too. I'll wait while you come around.

   Here's the thing: Generously soaking these cakes as they cool adds immense depth of flavor, and the additional moisture (read booze) keeps them fresh for days, to say nothing of weeks and months. The catch: Some of these cakes pack a punch, so you might want to designate a driver to take you home.

191	LAURA AND ADAM'S WEDDING CAKE
193	STICKY TOFFEE DATE CAKES
197	STOUT CAKE
199	POACHED APRICOT SACHERTORTE
203	CHOCOLATE, CHERRY, AND ORANGE CAKE
206	JAMAICAN BLACK CAKE
209	FIG, PORT, AND CHOCOLATE CAKE
212	APRIGOJI MOCHANUT BREAKFAST LOAVES
214	POMEGRANATE MOLASSES AND CHERRY CAKE
218	FLAMING FIGGY PUDDING

LAURA AND ADAM'S WEDDING CAKE

| MAKES 8 TO 10 SERVINGS | EASY |

People often laugh when I tell them I surprised my brother and sister-in-law with a fruitcake for their wedding; they shouldn't. If you want to bake the big cake and be a part of the celebration, there's no better choice, as this cake only gets better with age. Laura and Adam got married in early October, so I made them something that screams fall with dried apples, pears, and pecans. It has just a touch of sugar (and a heavy dose of booze), which keeps the cake so moist you might mistake it for pudding.

FOR THE CAKE

Pan Goo (page 224), for greasing the pan		
all-purpose flour	½ cup	71 grams
ground ginger	1 teaspoon	2.8 grams
baking powder	½ teaspoon	1.5 grams
coarse salt	½ teaspoon	1.5 grams
freshly ground cardamom (see page 11)	½ teaspoon	1 gram
freshly grated nutmeg (see page 12)	5 seconds (about ¼ teaspoon)	0.5 gram
unsalted butter, softened	6 tablespoons (¾ stick)	85 grams
firmly packed dark brown sugar	½ cup	106 grams
large eggs	3	3
honey	2 tablespoons	40 grams
dried apples, roughly chopped in ½-inch pieces	1½ cups	100 grams
dried pears, roughly chopped in ½-inch pieces	1½ cups	200 grams
pecans, lightly toasted (see page 18) and broken into pieces	1 cup	110 grams

FOR THE COCKTAIL

bourbon	¼ cup (2 ounces)	62 milliliters
Campari	¼ cup (2 ounces)	62 milliliters
sweet vermouth	¼ cup (2 ounces)	62 milliliters
granulated sugar	1 teaspoon	4 grams

(continued)

whole milk, as needed	1 to 2 tablespoons	15 to 30 milliliters
confectioners' sugar	½ cup	57 grams
vanilla ice cream, for serving, optional		

1. Preheat the oven to 300°F (150°C) with a rack in the center position. Line the bottom of a 6 x 3-inch round cake pan (see below) with parchment and brush with Pan Goo.

2. In a small bowl, whisk together the flour, ginger, baking powder, salt, cardamom, and nutmeg. Set aside.

3. In the bowl of an electric mixer fitted with the paddle attachment, beat the butter and dark brown sugar on medium-high speed until well combined, 2 to 3 minutes. Add the eggs, one at a time, scraping down the bowl and beating well after each addition. Add the honey and beat on high speed until the mixture is foamy, about 4 minutes. Scrape down the sides of the bowl, add the dry ingredients, and mix on low speed until a very loose batter forms. Add the dried fruit and nuts, stirring to combine. It's a lot of fruit; I know. Scrape the batter into the prepared pan.

4. Bake until the cake is deep golden brown and springs back to the touch, about 90 minutes.

5. Transfer the pan to a wire rack set on a rimmed baking sheet. Allow the cake to cool in the pan for 10 minutes, then remove the cake to the rack. Use a wooden skewer to poke holes all the way from the top of the cake to the bottom, spaced about 1 inch apart, to help the cocktail absorb.

6. Prepare the cocktail by stirring together all the ingredients in a small measuring cup. Tip a tipple, then pour over the cooling cake a little at a time, allowing the mixture to soak all the way through to the center. It will seem like a lot of booze, but that's the point. Let the cake cool completely to room temperature.

7. Make the glaze and finish the cake the day you plan to serve it. Stir the milk into the confectioners' sugar a little at a time until the mixture just coats the back of a spoon. Spread the glaze over the top of the cake and let it drip down the sides. Serve with vanilla ice cream, if you must.

STORAGE

The soaked cake can be stored in an airtight container in a cool spot for a very long time; the flavors will actually get better with age. If you plan to keep the cake for more than 2 weeks, mix together a similar cocktail to brush over the cake from time to time—the alcohol will serve as a preservative.

MAKING DO

If you don't have a 3-inch-tall cake pan, you can get by with a standard 2-inch number. Line the sides with a 20-inch-long strip of parchment that is 3 inches wide, creating a collar that will contain the cake as it rises. Brush the collar with Pan Goo, too.

STICKY TOFFEE DATE CAKES

| MAKES 12 SMALL CAKES | EASY |

Here comes a two-fold sticky situation, by way of the golden syrup and the dates themselves, which break down in the rum soak to become just a fantasy of what they once were. Look for dates that are plump and clump together, as fresh as a dried fruit can be—they'll have the sweetest flavor to impart.

FOR THE CAKES

pitted dates, preferably Medjool, divided	1⅓ cups	257 grams
dark rum	2 tablespoons	30 milliliters
boiling water	½ cup	125 milliliters
Pan Goo (page 224), for greasing the pan		
pure vanilla extract	1 teaspoon	5 milliliters
unsalted butter, softened	4 tablespoons (½ stick)	57 grams
large egg	1	1
Lyle's Golden Syrup or honey	½ cup	175 grams
all-purpose flour	1 cup	142 grams
baking powder	1 teaspoon	3 grams
coarse salt	¾ teaspoon	2.3 grams

FOR THE TOFFEE SAUCE

unsalted butter	4 tablespoons (½ stick)	57 grams
firmly packed dark brown sugar	¼ cup	53 grams
coarse salt	1 pinch	1 pinch
heavy cream	¾ cup	187 milliliters
dark rum (or more, to taste)	2 tablespoons	30 milliliters

(continued)

1. In a small bowl, combine 1 cup (193 grams) of the dates with the rum and boiling water. Let the dates sit and absorb the liquid until they're falling apart, about 30 minutes. Roughly chop the remaining ⅓ cup (64 grams) of dates into ¼-inch pieces and set aside.

2. Preheat the oven to 350°F (180°C) with a rack in the center position. Brush a standard 12-cup muffin tin with Pan Goo.

3. In the bowl of a food processor, combine the soaked dates and any remaining liquid with the vanilla, butter, egg, and golden syrup. Pulse a few times to combine, then puree until the mixture is very smooth, about 1 minute. Add the flour, baking powder, and salt, and pulse four or five times, until a rich batter forms. Scrape the batter into a bowl and stir in the reserved chopped dates.

4. Evenly divide the batter among the wells of the prepared muffin tin, filling each well about halfway. Give the pan a couple of firm taps on the counter to level the batter.

5. Bake until the cakes are deep golden brown, spring back to the touch, and a cake tester inserted into the center comes out with moist crumbs, about 20 minutes.

6. Get to work on the sauce while the cakes are baking. In a small saucepan, combine the butter, dark brown sugar, and salt and set over medium-low heat, whisking constantly, until the butter melts. Continue whisking until the mixture is smooth and you can catch a glimpse of the bottom of the pan as you drag the whisk through, which will take a minute or so. Slowly stream in the cream, whisking away. Be mindful of the steam; it will be intense. Boil the mixture for about 6 minutes, whisking occasionally, until the sauce has thickened slightly and has taken on a light amber hue. Keep the sauce warm, but not hot, stirring occasionally until you're ready to use it. Whisk in the rum just before serving.

7. As soon as the cakes come out of the oven, spoon a tablespoon or two of sauce over each and let it soak in before removing the cakes from the pan. Serve the cakes warm with the remaining sauce passed on the side, or transfer the cakes to a wire rack, glaze generously, and serve at room temperature. In either case, serve them today (please).

STORAGE

These cakes are best freshly made and still warm from the oven. Leftovers can be loosely covered and stored at room temperature overnight. Refrigerate any remaining sauce.

TIMING IS EVERYTHING

If you want these cakes piping hot when you're ready to serve dessert, mix the batter just before your guests arrive and portion the dough into the muffin pan. Loosely cover and keep at room temperature for an hour or two, waiting until you're nearly ready to serve before putting the pan in the oven. The sauce can also be made ahead and kept in the saucepan, off heat, for an hour or two. Warm it gently and whisk it vigorously to bring it back to life.

STOUT CAKE

Beer is a wonderful ingredient to bake with because it has the same complexities as any fermented product: a savoriness that comes from the yeast itself, the dry bitterness of the hops, and the sweetness of the malt and other grains added during the brew. The rich, chocolatey taste of stout lends itself particularly well to this cake, echoing the sweetness of the fruit and the spice of the candied ginger.

Beers are bottled in a variety of sizes, generally around 12 ounces each. Don't get too hung up on the measurements for the beer in the cake; anything approximating 1½ bottles will do—but make sure to save exactly ¾ cup (187 milliliters) for the frosting.

FOR THE CAKE

chopped dried tart cherries	1 cup	100 grams
coarsely chopped dried apricots	½ cup	90 grams
stout beer, divided	2 cups (16 ounces)	500 milliliters
Pan Goo (page 224), for greasing the pan		
all-purpose flour	2 cups	284 grams
baking powder	2 teaspoons	6 grams
ground cinnamon	2 teaspoons	5 grams
coarse salt	1½ teaspoons	4.5 grams
ground allspice	¾ teaspoon	1.5 grams
freshly grated nutmeg (see page 12)	10 seconds (about ½ teaspoon)	1 gram
unsalted butter, softened	1 cup (2 sticks)	226 grams
firmly packed dark brown sugar	1 cup	212 grams
granulated sugar	1 cup	212 grams
large eggs	4	4
pure vanilla extract	1 tablespoon	15 milliliters
candied ginger, finely chopped	½ cup	82 grams
pecans, lightly toasted (see page 18) and coarsely crumbled	1 cup	110 grams
coarsely chopped best-quality milk chocolate	1 cup	128 grams

SOAKED

(continued)   **197**

granulated sugar	¾ cup	159 grams
cornstarch	3 tablespoons	24 grams
coarse salt	1 pinch	1 pinch
stout beer	¾ cup (6 ounces)	187 milliliters
unsalted butter, softened	½ cup (1 stick)	113 grams
confectioners' sugar	1 cup	113 grams

1. Combine the cherries and apricots in a large bowl and cover with 1½ cups (375 milliliters) of beer. They've had a long day and they deserve it. Cover the bowl and let them soak for about 4 hours, or overnight if you're feeling generous.

2. Preheat the oven to 325°F (170°C) with a rack in the center position. Generously brush a 9 x 2-inch square cake pan with Pan Goo.

3. In a small bowl, whisk together the flour, baking powder, cinnamon, salt, allspice, and nutmeg. Set aside.

4. In the bowl of an electric mixer fitted with the paddle attachment, beat the butter and both sugars on medium speed until the mixture is light and creamy, about 2 minutes. Scrape down the sides of the bowl and add the eggs, one at a time, beating well after each, and scraping, well, occasionally. Add the vanilla and continue beating until the mixture is very light and fluffy, about 3 minutes, then scrape down the bowl again.

5. Add the flour mixture and stir on low speed until just combined. Add the soaked fruit and any remaining beer, the candied ginger, pecans, and chocolate. Stir on low speed until the fruit and nuts are evenly distributed. Scrape the batter into the prepared pan and smooth the top with an offset spatula.

6. Bake the cake until the top springs back to the touch and a cake tester comes out with moist crumbs, 75 to 80 minutes.

7. Remove the pan from the oven. Use a wooden skewer to poke holes all the way down to the bottom of the cake, spaced about 1 inch apart. Pour the remaining ½ cup (125 milliliters) of beer over the cake and let it cool completely in the pan.

8. To make the frosting, whisk the granulated sugar, cornstarch, and salt together in a small saucepan. Slowly add the stout while whisking constantly. Take care to break up any lumps of cornstarch. Bring the mixture to a boil over medium heat, whisking constantly. Continue cooking and whisking until the mixture is thick and rather gluey, about 6 minutes. Pour into a heatproof bowl and cover with a piece of plastic film or wax paper. Set aside until completely cool or refrigerate overnight (but return to room temperature before using).

9. In the bowl of an electric mixer fitted with the paddle attachment, combine the butter and confectioners' sugar. Begin mixing on low speed until all the sugar has been absorbed, then beat on medium speed until light, about 2 minutes. Stop the mixer and scrape down the sides of the bowl. Add the cooled beer "pudding" and beat on medium-high speed until very light and fluffy, about 2 minutes.

10. Frost the cake. Cut into 9 slices. Do a jig.

STORAGE

The cake will keep in the refrigerator, loosely covered, for up to 2 days. Bring to room temperature before serving.

POACHED APRICOT SACHERTORTE

| MAKES 8 TO 10 SERVINGS | ADVANCED |

The original Sachertort, which hails from Vienna, was designed to be shipped to admirers on the other side of the world. Mine is meant for admirers on the other side of your table. I've gussied it up with fresh apricots poached in aromatic spices. There's something romantic about the way it all melds together . . . maybe that's why we talk about flavors marrying.

FOR THE POACHED APRICOTS

granulated sugar	2 cups	424 grams
vanilla bean, split lengthwise and seeds scraped out	1	1
pure almond extract	2 teaspoons	10 milliliters
fresh ginger, thinly sliced	2 inches	30 grams
green cardamom pods, cracked	4	4
firm-ripe fresh apricots, halved and pitted	6	272 grams
brandy	1 tablespoon	15 milliliters

FOR THE SPICED CHOCOLATE CAKE

Pan Goo (page 224), for greasing the pan		
all-purpose flour	¾ cup	107 grams
coarse salt	1 teaspoon	3 grams
freshly ground cardamom (see page 11)	1 teaspoon	2 grams
ground cinnamon	1 teaspoon	2.5 grams
ground aniseed (see page 202)	½ teaspoon	1 gram
large eggs, separated	6	6
granulated sugar	½ cup	106 grams
unsalted butter, softened	¾ cup (1½ sticks)	170 grams
confectioners' sugar	1½ cups	170 grams
best-quality bittersweet chocolate, preferably around 65% cacao, melted and cooled	8 ounces	227 grams
pure vanilla extract	1 tablespoon	15 milliliters

(continued)

best-quality bittersweet chocolate, preferably around 65% cacao, finely chopped	4 ounces	113 grams
honey	1 tablespoon	20 grams
heavy cream	½ cup	125 milliliters
thinly sliced dried apricots tossed with granulated sugar, for garnish		

1. Make the poaching liquid by combining the granulated sugar, vanilla bean and seeds, almond extract, ginger, cardamom pods, and 2 cups (500 milliliters) of water in a small saucepan. Bring to a boil over high heat and cook, stirring occasionally, until the sugar dissolves, about 2 minutes. Reduce the temperature until just barely simmering and add the apricots, working in batches as space allows. Cook until the fruit is knife-tender but not falling apart, 7 to 10 minutes, and use a slotted spoon to transfer them to a heatproof bowl. When all the apricots have been poached, drown them in the poaching syrup and refrigerate for up to 3 days, until you're ready to assemble the cake.

2. Preheat the oven to 350°F (180°C) with a rack in the center position. Brush two 9 x 2-inch round cake pans with Pan Goo and line the bottoms with parchment.

3. Whisk together the flour, salt, and spices in a small bowl and set aside.

4. In the bowl of an electric mixer fitted with the whisk attachment, begin whipping the egg whites on medium speed. Gradually shake the granulated sugar into the bowl while slowly increasing the speed to high. Continue whipping until stiff peaks form, about 3 minutes. Scrape the beaten egg whites into a bowl and set aside while you put together the rest of the batter.

5. Place the butter, confectioners' sugar, and melted chocolate in the mixer bowl and switch to the paddle attachment. Beat until well combined, about 2 minutes. Scrape down the sides of the bowl more frequently than you might otherwise care to as you add the egg yolks, one at a time, followed by the vanilla, mixing on medium speed until creamy and smooth. Sift the flour mixture over the batter and fold with a rubber spatula until just combined.

6. Stir about a third of the beaten egg whites into the batter to lighten, then gently fold in the remaining whites in two additions. Divide the batter into the prepared pans and smooth the tops with an offset spatula.

7. Bake the cakes until they are firm, spring back to the touch, and a cake tester comes out clean, about 25 minutes.

8. Transfer the pans to wire racks. Let the cakes rest in the pans for 15 minutes, then run a knife around the edges to loosen them. Invert the cakes onto the racks to cool completely. The sides of the cakes will be crumbly. Brush off the crumbs and eat them as a snack.

9. Meanwhile, drain the apricots—save the syrup!—and discard the vanilla bean and cardamom pods. Cut half of the apricots into ¼-inch-thick slices; set them aside. Return the remaining apricots, ¼ cup (62 milliliters) of the syrup, and the brandy to a small saucepan. Cook. Mash. Stir. After 2 to 3 minutes, when the fruit has broken down into a jammy puree, strain it through a coarse-mesh sieve to remove the peels. Set aside.

10. Brush one cake layer with about 3 tablespoons of the poaching syrup. Spread about

(continued)

half the apricot puree over the cake and nestle the sliced apricots on top. Brush the second cake layer with another 3 tablespoons of syrup and place on top of the apricots. (Save the remaining syrup for cocktails.) Using an offset spatula, smear the remaining apricot puree over the top and sides of the cake to thinly coat. Refrigerate the cake while you make the glaze.

11. Place the chopped chocolate and honey in a small heatproof bowl. In a small saucepan, heat the cream until bubbles form around just the edge of the pan. Pour the cream over the chocolate and stand idly by as it softens, then vigorously stir the mixture with a rubber spatula until it forms a smooth ganache.

12. Pour the glaze over the top of the cake and spread over the edges with a large spatula, letting it drip down and coat the sides. Chill the cake until the ganache sets, about 20 minutes or up to 1 day. Garnish with sugared dried apricots.

STORAGE

You can keep the cake in the refrigerator for 3 or 4 days, but if you love me at all, bring it to room temperature before serving.

MAKING DO

If fresh apricots are hard to find, you can substitute 3 firm-ripe peaches.

GROUND ANISEED

Aniseed is so small it can be hard to grind in a spice grinder. I find a mortar and pestle does the trick nicely.

CHOCOLATE, CHERRY, AND ORANGE CAKE

| MAKES 8 TO 10 SERVINGS | EASY |

In another life, this might have been a Black Forest Cake, but it didn't work out that way. Here's how it did work out: Rich, decadent, and quite frankly improved. Sweet, tart, and fudgy. It's basically a grown-up brownie, and it comes together just as easily.

The cake will keep in an airtight container for what seems like forever, but if you leave it on your counter it probably won't survive a day.

FOR THE CAKE

unsweetened dried tart cherries	⅔ cup	67 grams
orange liqueur, such as Triple Sec	2 tablespoons	30 milliliters
boiling water	2 tablespoons	30 milliliters
unsalted butter, cut into ½-inch pieces, plus additional softened for greasing the pan	½ cup (1 stick)	113 grams
unsweetened cocoa powder, preferably Dutch-processed, plus additional for dusting the pan	3 tablespoons	15 grams
all-purpose flour	⅔ cup	95 grams
baking powder	½ teaspoon	1.5 grams
coarse salt	½ teaspoon	1.5 grams
roughly chopped best-quality semisweet chocolate, around 60% cacao	1⅓ cups	171 grams
cherry preserves	¾ cup	240 grams
firmly packed light brown sugar	⅔ cup	141 grams
finely grated orange zest (from 1 orange)	2 teaspoons	4 grams
large eggs	3	3

FOR FINISHING

freshly squeezed orange juice (from ½ orange)	2 tablespoons	30 milliliters
orange liqueur, such as Triple Sec	1 tablespoon	15 milliliters

(continued)

SOAKED

1. Roughly chop the dried cherries. I know that the idea of doing so is obnoxious, but if you don't, the cake will be difficult to serve. Grin, bear it, and thank me later. When that's settled, combine the cherries with the orange liqueur and boiling water in a small bowl. Let the cherries sit to absorb as much liquid as possible while you get on with the rest.

2. Preheat the oven to 350°F (180°C) with a rack in the center position. Generously butter an 8 x 2-inch round cake pan and line the bottom with parchment. Butter the parchment, too, then dust the pan with cocoa powder, tapping out any excess.

3. In a small bowl, whisk together the flour, cocoa powder, baking powder, and salt.

4. In a large heatproof bowl, combine the butter and chocolate and set over a pan of gently simmering water. Stir the mixture with a rubber spatula until almost completely melted, then remove the bowl from the heat and stir until no lumps remain. Whisk in the cherry preserves, light brown sugar, and orange zest. Add the eggs, one at a time, mixing vigorously until a rich batter forms. Stir in the dry ingredients with a rubber spatula until just combined. Gently fold in the reserved cherries and any remaining liquid and pour the batter into the prepared pan.

5. Bake until the cake springs back to the touch and a cake tester inserted into the center comes out with moist crumbs, about 50 minutes.

6. Transfer the pan to a wire rack. Let the cake cool in the pan for just a few minutes before unmolding it onto the rack.

7. In a small bowl, stir together the orange juice and liqueur. Brush the cake with the mixture while it's still warm; it will absorb more than you think. Serve the cake in small slices. Save room for seconds.

STORAGE

The cake will keep for at least 3 days in an airtight container at room temperature.

JAMAICAN BLACK CAKE

| MAKES ABOUT 10 SERVINGS | EASY | OVERNIGHT |

This Jamaican fruitcake gets its color from burnt sugar syrup, which imparts an intensely dark flavor that can't easily be replicated. It can be found online and in specialty stores, but if you're having trouble locating it, extra-dark blackstrap molasses makes a passable (though less nuanced) alternative.

FOR THE FRUIT MIXTURE

unsweetened dried tart cherries	½ cup	50 grams
prunes, roughly chopped	½ cup	92 grams
dark raisins	½ cup	80 grams
orange Candied Citrus Peel (page 236), cut into ¼-inch pieces	½ cup	90 grams
dried currants	¼ cup	35 grams
dark rum	¼ cup	62 milliliters

FOR THE CAKE

Pan Goo (page 224), for greasing the pan		
all-purpose flour	1 cup	142 grams
baking powder	1 teaspoon	3 grams
coarse salt	½ teaspoon	1.5 grams
ground cinnamon	1 teaspoon	2.5 grams
ground allspice	½ teaspoon	1 gram
ground cloves	¼ teaspoon	0.6 gram
freshly grated nutmeg (see page 12)	5 seconds (about ¼ teaspoon)	0.5 gram
ground mace (see page 77)	¼ teaspoon	1.2 grams
unsalted butter, softened	½ cup (1 stick)	113 grams
firmly packed dark brown sugar	¾ cup	159 grams
large eggs	2	2
pure vanilla extract	2 teaspoons	10 milliliters
burnt sugar syrup or blackstrap molasses	¼ cup	90 grams
walnuts, lightly toasted (see page 18) and broken into halves and pieces	¾ cup	77 grams
dark rum, plus additional for aging the cakes	⅓ cup	83 milliliters

(continued)

FRUIT CAKE

1. In a large bowl, combine the ingredients for the fruit mixture, stirring well to make sure none of it will pass a sobriety test. Cover the bowl and set it aside in a cool, dark place for at least one night or up to 1 week.

2. Preheat the oven to 300°F (150°C) with a rack in the center position. Grease a standard 8½ x 4½-inch loaf pan with Pan Goo.

3. In a small bowl, whisk together the flour, baking powder, salt, and spices. Set aside.

4. Using an electric mixer fitted with the paddle attachment, beat the butter and dark brown sugar on medium-high speed until light and fluffy, about 3 minutes. Scrape down the sides of the bowl and add the eggs, one at a time, mixing well after each addition. Scrape down the bowl again and add the vanilla and burnt sugar syrup. The batter will appear broken at first. Slowly increase the mixer speed to high and continue beating for 3 to 5 minutes to incorporate as much air as possible into the batter. Stop the mixer and scrape down the bowl for what will feel like the eight thousandth time.

5. Pause to contemplate whoever invented the spatula and remember to thank them later.

Add the flour mixture and mix on low speed until combined, then add the soaked fruit and toasted walnuts, stirring gently by hand to evenly distribute them into the batter. Scrape the batter into the prepared pan and smooth the top with a small offset spatula.

6. Bake until the cake springs back to the touch and a cake tester inserted into the center comes out clean, about 1 hour and 45 minutes.

7. Transfer the pan to a wire rack. Pour the rum evenly over the cake, letting it soak all the way down to its nether regions. Allow the cake to cool completely in the pan.

STORAGE

It would be a real shame not to age this cake for at least a week by wrapping it in cheesecloth and brushing with more rum. Place the wrapped cake in an airtight container and check on it periodically, brushing the cheesecloth with additional rum whenever it seems dry. A cake stored with this much care (to say nothing of the booze) will last very well.

THE MORE THE MERRIER

For those of us in the know, aged cakes make great gifts. You can easily double this recipe if you'd like to save one cake for yourself.

FIG, PORT, AND CHOCOLATE CAKE

| MAKES 8 TO 10 SERVINGS | EASY | OVERNIGHT |
| SPECIAL EQUIPMENT: 6-CUP BUNDT PAN |

If you've ever turned a casual stalker into a newfound friend, you should meet my friend Linda. She was alone in Porto when she noticed two figures following her. They were everywhere she was and only sometimes where she wasn't. She wondered if they were after her kidneys or just her itinerary as she finally turned to face them.

You may have guessed that they were after neither.* Happily, the three went wine tasting and together discovered a bottle of port that was so deep and fruity it was bursting with the aromas of sun-dried figs and chocolate. Linda left me that bottle when she departed New York to join the United Nations in Afghanistan, because she's a better person than I am.

FOR THE CAKE

dried figs, stemmed and coarsely chopped	2 cups	380 grams
tawny port	1 cup	250 milliliters
Pan Goo (page 224), for greasing the pan		
all-purpose flour	1¼ cups	178 grams
baking powder	1 teaspoon	3 grams
coarse salt	¾ teaspoon	2.3 grams
unsalted butter, softened	6 tablespoons (¾ stick)	85 grams
granulated sugar	1 cup	212 grams
large eggs	3	3
pure vanilla extract	2 teaspoons	10 milliliters
pecans, lightly toasted (see page 18) and coarsely crumbled	1 cup	110 grams
coarsely chopped best-quality milk chocolate	1 cup	128 grams
coarsely chopped best-quality dark chocolate, preferably around 65% cacao	½ cup	64 grams

FOR THE SOAKER

tawny port	¼ cup	62 milliliters
firmly packed light brown sugar	2 tablespoons	27 grams

---

* In fact, they were hoping to practice their Mandarin.

(continued)

finely chopped best-quality dark chocolate, preferably around 65% cacao	½ cup	64 grams
heavy cream	2 tablespoons	30 milliliters
tawny port	2 tablespoons	30 milliliters
unsalted butter, softened	1 tablespoon	14 grams
coarse salt	1 pinch	1 pinch

1. Combine the figs and port in a small bowl. Cover and leave them for at least 12 hours at room temperature. Don't peek; it's impolite to watch.

2. Preheat the oven to 350°F (180°C) with a rack in the lower third position. Brush a 6-cup Bundt pan with Pan Goo, making sure you get into all the nooks and crannies.

3. In a small bowl, whisk together the flour, baking powder, and salt. Set aside.

4. In the bowl of an electric mixer fitted with the paddle attachment, beat the butter and granulated sugar on medium speed until the butter is extra light and fluffy, about 5 minutes. Scrape down the sides of the bowl and add the eggs, one at a time, beating well after each addition, then add the vanilla and beat to combine.

5. Add the flour mixture and stir on low speed until just combined, then stir in the pecans, both chocolates, the soaked figs, and any of the port that wasn't absorbed by the figs. Scrape the batter into the prepared Bundt pan.

6. Bake until a cake tester comes out clean, about 75 minutes, tenting with foil if the top darkens too quickly.

7. Remove the pan from the oven. Let the cake cool in the pan for 30 minutes before unmolding it onto a serving platter.

8. Make the soaker: In a small saucepan, combine the port and light brown sugar. Heat gently over low, stirring constantly until the sugar dissolves. Brush over the cooling cake.

9. When the cake is completely cool, make the glaze by combining the chocolate, cream, port, butter, and salt in a small heatproof bowl. Set the bowl over a pan of gently simmering water and heat just until the chocolate begins to melt, stirring often. Remove the bowl from the heat and stir vigorously until the chocolate has completely melted and a rich ganache forms. Spoon the glaze over the cake, letting it drip and pool.

STORAGE

The cake will keep at room temperature, covered, for the better part of a week, depending on how many guests you receive.

SOAKED

APRIGOJI MOCHANUT BREAKFAST LOAVES

Meant to be shared, not squandered, these cakes make excellent gifts, easily surviving the six-hour drive to visit those friends who only yesterday promised never to leave New York. I'm not angry; I'm just disappointed.

FOR THE LOAVES

dried apricots, roughly chopped	1 cup	180 grams
goji berries	½ cup	50 grams
dark rum	⅓ cup	83 milliliters
raw hazelnuts	1 cup	128 grams
unsalted butter, melted and cooled, plus additional for greasing the pans	6 tablespoons (¾ stick)	85 grams
unsweetened cocoa powder, preferably Dutch-processed, plus additional for dusting the pans	2 tablespoons	10 grams
all-purpose flour	1¾ cups	249 grams
coarse salt	1 teaspoon	3 grams
baking powder	1 teaspoon	3 grams
baking soda	¼ teaspoon	1.5 grams
finely ground coffee	2 teaspoons	2 grams
sour cream	¼ cup	61 grams
granulated sugar	¾ cup	159 grams
firmly packed light brown sugar	1 cup	212 grams
large eggs	3	3
whole milk	⅓ cup	83 milliliters

FOR THE SOAKER

dark rum	¼ cup	62 milliliters

1. Place the apricots, goji berries, and rum in a small bowl. Give them a quick toss to coat, then let the fruit sit for about an hour to absorb some of the booze.

2. Preheat the oven to 350°F (180°C) with a rack in the center position.

3. Place the hazelnuts on a rimmed baking sheet and toast until the skins begin to crack, 10 to 12

FRUIT CAKE

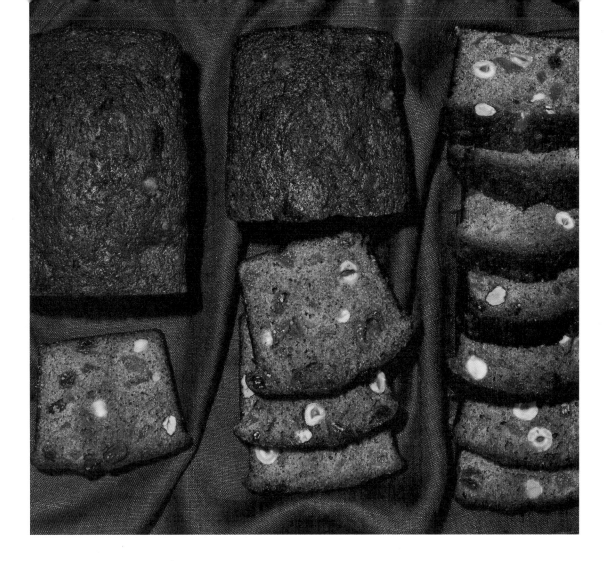

minutes. Gather the nuts in a clean kitchen towel and let them sit for a minute or so to cool slightly, then rub the nuts in the towel to dislodge the skins. Set aside.

4. Brush three 3¼ x 5¾ x 2¼-inch mini loaf pans with butter and dust with cocoa powder, tapping out the excess.

5. In a medium bowl, whisk together the flour, cocoa powder, salt, baking powder, baking soda, and coffee. Set aside.

6. In a large bowl, whisk together the melted butter, sour cream, and both sugars. Have at it until the mixture is thick and creamy, then whisk in the eggs one at a time. Whisk in half the dry ingredients, followed by the milk. Stir in the remaining dry ingredients, the soaked fruit and any remaining rum, and the hazelnuts.

7. Divide the batter into the pans and place the pans on a baking sheet. They will be very full. Bake the loaves until they are firm to the touch and a cake tester inserted into the centers comes out clean, about 52 minutes.

8. Transfer the pans to a wire rack. Allow the loaves to cool in the pans for 15 minutes before unmolding onto the rack. Brush the loaves with the rum soaker, then let cool completely. Serve gently toasted slices with butter for a breakfast treat.

STORAGE

Wrapped well, these loaves will keep for a week at room temperature or can be frozen for up to 3 months (or until you've forgotten where you put them).

POMEGRANATE MOLASSES AND CHERRY CAKE

| DAIRY-FREE | MAKES 9 TO 12 SERVINGS | EASY |

Substituting pomegranate molasses for the garden-variety kind imparts an exotic, bright sweetness to this dark, dense cake. It practically dances across your tongue. Scanning the ingredients, you may recognize it for what it is: gingerbread, but not that of the cookie-cutout persuasion.

FOR THE CAKE

dried sweet cherries, such as Bing	1 cup	100 grams
pomegranate molasses	¾ cup	242 grams
pomegranate juice	½ cup	125 milliliters
freshly grated ginger	1 tablespoon	15 grams
neutral oil, such as safflower, plus more for greasing the pan	¾ cup	187 milliliters
all-purpose flour	2 cups	284 grams
ground ginger	1 tablespoon	8.4 grams
ground cinnamon	2 teaspoons	5 grams
ground allspice	1 teaspoon	2 grams
ground black pepper	½ teaspoon	1.2 grams
baking soda	½ teaspoon	3 grams
coarse salt	½ teaspoon	1.5 grams
large eggs	2	2
firmly packed light brown sugar	¾ cup	159 grams

FOR THE COCKTAIL

pomegranate juice	2 tablespoons (1 ounce)	30 milliliters
white rum	2 tablespoons (1 ounce)	30 milliliters
orange liqueur, such as Triple Sec	2 tablespoons (1 ounce)	30 milliliters

FOR SERVING

vanilla ice cream, optional

(continued)

1. Roughly chop the dried cherries. (Having already apologized for asking you to do so on page 205, I will offer this consolation: for a modest fee, I will come over and chop your cherries for you.* What a difference it makes!)

2. In a small saucepan, combine the cherries, pomegranate molasses, juice, and ginger. Heat until bubbles form around the edge of the pan, stirring to dissolve the molasses. Set aside to cool.

3. Preheat the oven to 325°F (170°C). Brush an 8 x 2-inch square glass or ceramic baking dish with safflower oil.

4. In a medium bowl, whisk together the flour, ginger, cinnamon, allspice, pepper, baking soda, and salt.

5. In a large bowl, whisk together the oil, eggs, and light brown sugar until a creamy mixture forms. Whisk in the cooled pomegranate mixture, then stir in the dry ingredients with a rubber spatula.

6. Pour the batter into the prepared baking dish and bake for 1 hour, or until a cake tester inserted into the center comes out clean.

7. Meanwhile, make the cocktail by stirring together the pomegranate juice, white rum, and orange liqueur.

8. As soon as the cake comes out of the oven, use a wooden skewer to punch holes all the way through to the bottom, spaced about 1 inch apart. Slowly pour the cocktail over the cooling cake.

9. Allow the cake to cool in the baking dish. Serve with vanilla ice cream, if you'd like.

STORAGE

The cake will keep at room temperature, covered, for up to 3 days.

---

* I just heard how that sounds.

FLAMING FIGGY PUDDING

| MAKES 8 TO 10 SERVINGS | INTERMEDIATE |
| SPECIAL EQUIPMENT: 5-CUP PUDDING MOLD, PRESSURE COOKER |

I didn't grow up with steamed pudding, but I'm making up for lost time. I also didn't grow up with a pressure cooker. I have one now, and while it can be a bit gimmicky, using it for steamed pudding seems like a no-brainer. Many steamed puddings cook for 5 or more hours; even including the time it takes the machine to reach—and release—pressure, this is a lot faster. It's also truly self-sufficient. You never have to check that the water hasn't evaporated, and if you don't feel like pulling it out of the water bath the minute the valve clicks down, nothing terrible will happen. It could happily lounge in that Jacuzzi for hours.

Flaming anything is terrifyingly impressive, but if you can't get up the courage, this pudding tastes just as good when it's not on fire.

FOR THE STEAMED PUDDING

dried figs, stemmed and coarsely chopped	1 cup	190 grams
dried currants	⅓ cup	46 grams
dark rum	3 ounces	90 milliliters
unsalted butter, softened, plus more for the pan	4 tablespoons (½ stick)	57 grams
all-purpose flour	1 cup	142 grams
ground cinnamon	2 teaspoons	5 grams
coarse salt	1 teaspoon	3 grams
baking powder	½ teaspoon	1.5 grams
freshly grated nutmeg (see page 12)	10 seconds (about ½ teaspoon)	1 gram
ground cloves	1 pinch	1 pinch
firmly packed light brown sugar	¾ cup	159 grams
sour cream	¼ cup	61 grams
large eggs	2	2
finely grated orange zest (from 1 orange)	2 teaspoons	4 grams
pure vanilla extract	1 tablespoon	15 milliliters
finely chopped orange Candied Citrus Peel (page 236)	¼ cup	45 grams
lightly toasted (see page 18) and coarsely chopped pecans	½ cup	55 grams

(continued)

firmly packed light brown sugar	½ cup	106 grams
unsalted butter	2 tablespoons	28 grams
coarse salt	1 pinch	1 pinch

| rum (around 80 proof; see page 221) | 1 to 2 ounces | 30 to 60 milliliters |

1. In a small saucepan, combine the figs, currants, rum, and 1 cup (250 milliliters) water. Bring to a boil over medium heat, about 5 minutes. Remove from the heat and let the dried fruit soak for about 20 minutes.

2. Generously butter a 5-cup (1.25 liter) pudding mold.

3. In a small bowl, whisk together the flour, cinnamon, salt, baking powder, nutmeg, and cloves.

4. In a large bowl, beat the light brown sugar, butter, and sour cream with a rubber spatula until creamy. Add the eggs, one at a time, and mix well until smooth. Stir in the orange zest and vanilla. Stir in the dry ingredients until just combined. Drain the figs and currants, reserving the liquid. Gently fold the figs, currants, candied orange peel, and pecans into the batter. Scrape the batter into the pudding mold and firmly attach the lid.*

5. Place a small wire rack inside a pressure cooker. If your pudding mold does not have a built-in handle, create a sling by folding a long piece of foil in thirds to form a narrow, sturdy band about three times as long as the pudding mold is tall. Place the pudding mold (on this sling, if using) on top of the wire rack. Fill the pressure cooker with water to about 1 inch below the lip of the pudding dish, or to the maximum fill line, whichever is lower.

6. Seal the pressure cooker and bring to high pressure. Cook for 45 minutes, then let the pressure release naturally, about 1 hour, before opening.

7. Meanwhile, make the sauce. In a small saucepan, combine about ½ cup (125 milliliters) of the reserved soaking liquid, the light brown sugar, butter, and salt. Bring to a boil over medium heat and cook, stirring frequently, until it's sudsy and reduced to approximately ½ cup (125 milliliters), about 15 minutes. You should be able to catch a glimpse of the bottom of the pot when a spoon is dragged through the mixture. Keep the sauce warm, vigorously whisking on occasion, until ready to serve.

8. Carefully remove the pudding mold from the water bath and open the lid. The pudding should be very firm to the touch. Use a thin metal spatula to coax the cake away from the sides in a few places, then invert the mold onto a serving platter and give it a firm tap. The pudding should slide out easily.

9. To flambée the figgy pudding, place the rum in a small saucepan and warm over medium-low heat until you can just begin to smell the alcohol, a little less than 1 minute. Carefully transfer to a flameproof vessel with a handle and pour spout,

* Some pudding molds, ceramic ones for instance, don't have lids. In that case, cover the mold with a piece of buttered foil held firmly in place with a piece of kitchen twine.

such as a sturdy glass measuring cup. Dim the lights.

10. Tableside, and with care, use a grill lighter or long match to light the rum on fire, then ladle or pour the flaming rum over the cake. You don't need to use it all at once.

11. Smother the flames in the measuring cup with the lid of a small pot if you've had quite enough.

The cake should extinguish itself after about 10 glorious seconds.

12. Serve the cake warm or at room temperature with the sauce passed on the side.

STORAGE

The cake will keep, wrapped well, for a day or two at room temperature.

FLAMES ON THE SIDE OF MY FACE

It goes without saying that flambée-ing, well, *anything* should not be done by the faint of heart. What follows are some incontrovertible rules of thumb. You can never be too careful.

- Keep children, animals, exuberant gesticulators, and basically anything readily flammable at bay.

- Less is more. Two ounces (¼ cup) of alcohol is more than enough to impress.

- Never pour alcohol directly from the bottle into a cooking vessel; flames can travel and ignite the liquid in the bottle, shattering it. Use a small pitcher with a handle, such as a sturdy glass measuring cup instead. Clean up spills before setting anything on fire.

- A serving platter with a pronounced lip will contain the alcohol (and the flames).

- Never attempt to carry anything that is on fire. Set the booze alight and pour it over the cake tableside—close enough that the guests will oooh, far enough that they won't sue.

- Have a large metal bowl on hand to cover the cake and smother the flames. Just in case.

THE BASICS

The recipes and tips in this chapter are anything but supplemental. They're used throughout the book as component pieces or building blocks. They're also perfect springboards for your own creative pursuits. Do with them what you will.

224	PAN GOO
227	LADYFINGERS
228	PERFECT CHIFFON CAKE
230	TANGY CREAM CHEESE FROSTING
233	SWISS MERINGUE BUTTERCREAM
234	PASTRY CREAM
236	CANDIED CITRUS PEEL
239	ANY BERRY JAM
241	PINEAPPLE JAM
242	CRANBERRY JAM
243	APPLESAUCE
244	GINGER CITRUS CURD
247	SPECIAL SKILLS

PAN GOO

I'll admit it: I've been a parchment fiend, and my careless use has added up to unthinkable amounts of kitchen trash. Keep this mix on hand for a quick lube and easy slide.

neutral oil, such as safflower	¼ cup	62 milliliters
all-purpose flour	⅓ cup	47 grams

In a small container with a lid, whisk the oil and flour together until combined. Brush onto baking pans in place of parchment paper or cooking spray.

STORAGE

Keep it in the fridge for a couple of weeks. A month seems like maybe too long.

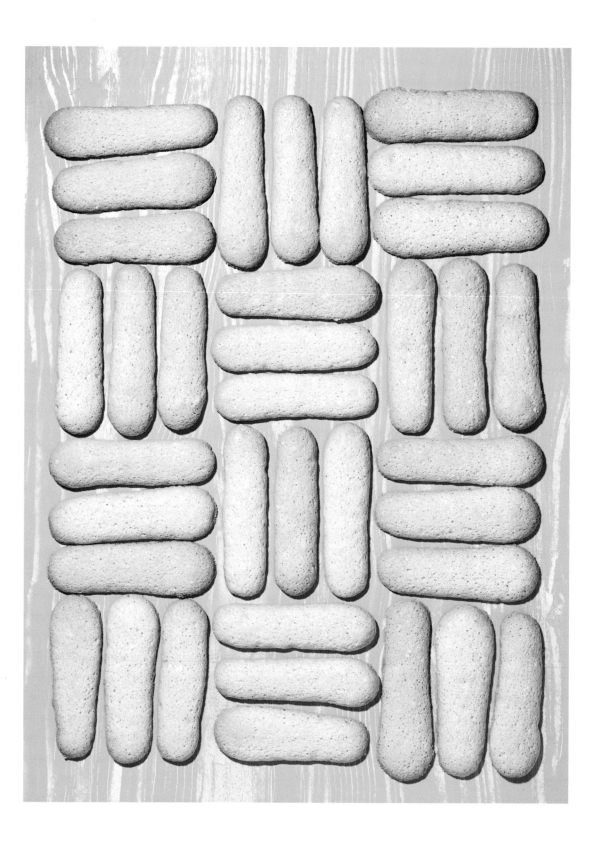

LADYFINGERS

| DAIRY-FREE | MAKES ABOUT THIRTY 3-INCH COOKIES | EASY |

These crispy cookies show up in the Banana Tiramisu (page 29), Strawberry Fools (page 111), and Kiwi and Goldenberry Saratoga Torte (page 146).

large eggs, separated	3	3
granulated sugar, divided	½ cup	106 grams
pure vanilla extract	1½ teaspoons	7.5 milliliters
coarse salt	½ teaspoon	1.5 grams
all-purpose flour	¾ cup	107 grams

1. Preheat the oven to 350°F (180° C) with racks in the lower third and middle positions. Line two 13 x 18-inch rimmed baking sheets with silicone baking mats or parchment paper.

2. Using an electric mixer fitted with the whisk attachment, whip the egg whites on medium speed until foamy. Gradually increase the speed of the mixer while slowly adding ¼ cup (53 grams) of sugar. When all the sugar is in the mix, continue whipping on high speed until firm peaks form, about 2 minutes longer. Scrape the meringue into a bowl and set aside.

3. Add the yolks, vanilla, salt, and remaining ¼ cup (53 grams) of sugar to the now-dirty mixer bowl and whip on high speed until the mixture is pale and thick, about 2 minutes. Stir about one third of the whipped egg whites into the yolk mixture to lighten, and then gently fold in the remaining egg whites in two additions.

4. Sift about a third of the flour over the batter through a fine-mesh sieve and gently fold until mostly combined. Sift and fold in the remaining flour in two additions.

5. If you're feeling fussy, transfer the batter to a piping bag fitted with a ½-inch plain round tip and pipe 3-inch-long cookies about 1 inch apart on the prepared baking sheets. If you're feeling unscrupulous, use a couple of spoons or a spring-loaded scoop to drop 2-tablespoon (30-milliliter) mounds of batter; they won't be fingers, but it will be okay.

6. Bake for 12 to 14 minutes, until the cookies spring back when gently pressed, rotating and transposing the baking sheets halfway. Reduce the temperature to 175°F (80°C) and continue baking for 20 minutes, opening the oven periodically to blow off some steam, or until the cookies are quite firm to the touch.

7. Remove the baking sheets from the oven and allow the ladyfingers to cool completely on them; the cookies will crisp up as they cool.

STORAGE

Store the ladyfingers at room temperature in an airtight container for a week or more.

PERFECT CHIFFON CAKE

| MAKES TWO 8-INCH CAKE LAYERS OR ONE 13 X 18-INCH SHEET CAKE FOR A ROULADE | INTERMEDIATE |

Chiffon cake sounds fussy, but if you follow my lead, you'll see it's actually quite easy to throw together. You'll use this recipe in the Key Lime Cake (page 112) and Cranberry Yule Log (page 125).

Pan Goo (page 224), for greasing the pan		
cake flour	1½ cups	170 grams
coarse salt	½ teaspoon	1.5 grams
baking soda	¼ teaspoon	1.5 grams
large eggs, separated	6	6
granulated sugar, divided	1 cup	212 grams
pure vanilla extract	1 tablespoon	15 milliliters
neutral oil, such as safflower	¼ cup	62 milliliters
buttermilk	½ cup	125 milliliters
confectioners' sugar, for dusting (if you're making a roulade)		

1. Preheat the oven to 350°F (180°C) and select your pans. For round layers, use two 8 x 2-inch round cake pans brushed with Pan Goo. For a roulade, use a 13 x 18-inch rimmed baking sheet lined with a silicone baking mat or parchment paper and brushed with Pan Goo.

2. In a small bowl, whisk together the flour, salt, and baking soda. Set aside.

3. In a large bowl, place the egg yolks and whisk in ½ cup (106 grams) of the granulated sugar, the vanilla, oil, and buttermilk. Set aside.

4. Using an electric mixer fitted with the whisk attachment, whip the egg whites on a healthy medium speed. When they look good and frothy, shake in the remaining ½ cup (106 grams) of the granulated sugar a little at a time, while slowly increasing the mixer speed to high. Keep whipping until the egg whites reach sturdy but not firm peaks.

5. Here's where all your organization pays off. Grab the dry ingredients and whisk them into the yolk mixture. Make sure there are no lumps; nobody likes that. Then use a large rubber spatula to scoop about a third of the whipped egg whites into the batter and whisk to lighten the mixture. Bakers call this a "sacrifice," so do it with dignity. Add the rest of the egg whites in two additions, folding gently until just combined.

FOR ROUND LAYERS

6. Divide the batter evenly into the two prepared pans, filling each about halfway.

7. Bake until the cakes are golden brown and spring back excitedly when gently pressed and a

cake tester inserted into the centers comes out clean, about 25 minutes.

8. Transfer the pans to wire racks. Let the cakes rest in their pans for about 2 minutes, then carefully flip them out onto the racks. (You'll be surprised by how easily they drop from the pans.) Turn them right side up on the racks and let them cool completely.

FOR A ROULADE

6. Pour the batter into the prepared baking sheet and spread it evenly to the corners with an offset spatula.

7. Bake the roulade until the cake is golden brown and springs back in the center and a cake tester comes out clean, about 16 minutes.

8. When the cake is in the oven, start worrying about how you're going to cool it. Clear off a substantial section of your counter and spread out a clean, lint-free kitchen towel (at least as big as the baking sheet). Sift a liberal amount confectioners' sugar over the towel.

9. When the cake is ready, run a knife around the edge of the pan. Invert onto the towel and remove the silicone baking mat or parchment. Dust the top with additional confectioners' sugar and, beginning at a short end, roll the cake and towel into a tight log.

10. Transfer the cake to a wire rack and let it cool completely.

STORAGE

The cooled cakes can be used immediately or wrapped and refrigerated for up to 2 days. Round layers can be frozen for up to 1 month. I wouldn't recommend freezing roulades, as they are apt to crack.

TANGY CREAM CHEESE FROSTING

| MAKES ABOUT 3 CUPS (820 GRAMS) | EASY |

The addition of crème fraîche to this frosting provides a tangy balance to the sweetness of the confectioners' sugar. Use a single recipe of this frosting to dress up the Pumpkin Cupcakes (page 71), and a double recipe for the Hummingbird Layer Cake (page 115).

cream cheese, softened	¾ cup (6 ounces)	170 grams
unsalted butter, softened	½ cup (1 stick)	113 grams
crème fraîche	2 tablespoons	30 grams
coarse salt	½ teaspoon	1.5 grams
confectioners' sugar	4½ cups (about 1¼ pounds)	about 500 grams

1. In the bowl of an electric mixer fitted with the paddle attachment, place the cream cheese, butter, crème fraîche, and salt. Beat on medium-high speed until the mixture is creamy, about 1 minute.

2. Stop the mixer and add about a third of the confectioners' sugar. Mix on low speed to prevent any sugar explosions, and then gradually increase the speed to high, beating for about 1 minute, until the mixture is light and airy.

3. Add the remaining confectioners' sugar in two additions in the same manner, stopping to scrape down the sides of the bowl occasionally, beating until the mixture is very light and smooth.

4. If the frosting is too soft to use immediately, refrigerate for about 15 minutes to firm it up.

STORAGE
Keep in an airtight container in the refrigerator for up to 1 week. Return to a cool room temperature before using.

INCREASING THE YIELD

This recipe can easily be doubled in one go; just be sure to add the sugar in 5 or 6 additions to ensure successful mixing.

SWISS MERINGUE BUTTERCREAM

| MAKES ABOUT 3 CUPS (500 GRAMS) | EASY |

This is my go-to frosting whenever I want luxurious swoops and swirls that can hold up to whatever life throws at it. You'll need one batch for the Cranberry Yule Log (page 125).

large egg whites	3	3
granulated sugar	¾ cup	159 grams
coarse salt	½ teaspoon	1.5 grams
unsalted butter, cut into 1-inch pieces and softened	1 cup (2 sticks)	226 grams
pure vanilla extract, optional	1 tablespoon	15 milliliters

1. Make the Swiss meringue: In the bowl of an electric mixer, whisk the egg whites, sugar, and salt until the sugar has been completely moistened. Place the bowl over a pan of gently simmering water and heat, whisking frequently, until the sugar dissolves and the mixture is hot to the touch (160°F, 71°C), about 3 minutes.

2. Transfer the bowl to the mixer fitted with the whisk attachment. Whip on high speed until the egg whites form stiff peaks and have cooled to just above body temperature, about 5 minutes.

3. Break the meringue: Reduce the mixer speed to medium and begin adding the butter, about 1 tablespoon (14 grams) at a time. The meringue will collapse as soon as the first bit of butter hits the foam. Continue adding the butter, a little at a time, waiting until the previous addition has more or less been eviscerated before continuing, 30 seconds or so should do it. The meringue will become droopy and soupy, but when all the butter has been added it will snap together, forming a luscious frosting. Scrape down the sides of the bowl and add the vanilla, if using.

4. Switch to the paddle attachment. Beat on low speed for about 1 minute to remove some of the larger air bubbles.

STORAGE

Unflavored buttercream can be stored in an airtight container at room temperature for up to 1 day or refrigerated for up to 1 week. Before using, bring to room temperature and beat lightly by hand or with an electric mixer fitted with the paddle attachment until smooth.

Buttercream that has been flavored with perishable items, such as fresh fruit or preserves, should be kept at room temperature for no more than a few hours, or stored in an airtight container in the refrigerator for up to 1 week.

FLAVORING BUTTERCREAM

You can easily flavor this buttercream with additional extracts, jam, or custards (as I do for the Cranberry Yule Log) by beating them in with the paddle attachment in step 4, above.

PASTRY CREAM

This is one of first techniques they teach in pastry school, and for good reason—it's almost endlessly versatile. Use it on its own or mix with nearly anything you have on hand for a foolproof filling. Use chilled Pastry Cream in the Strawberry Fools (page 111) and Guava Crepe Cake (page 141). You'll need a warm batch for the Raspberry Dacquoise Cake (page 132).

granulated sugar	½ cup	106 grams
cornstarch	3 tablespoons	24 grams
coarse salt	1 pinch	1 pinch
freshly grated nutmeg (see page 12)	10 seconds (about ½ teaspoon)	1 gram
large egg yolks	3	3
pure vanilla extract	2 teaspoons	10 milliliters
whole milk	1½ cups	375 milliliters

1. First off, set a fine-mesh sieve in a heatproof bowl. Then, in a small saucepan, whisk together the sugar, cornstarch, salt, and nutmeg. Whisk the egg yolks and vanilla into the dry mixture until it forms a lump-free paste.

2. Whisk in the milk, starting with just a few teaspoons, until the paste has loosened, then add the rest of the milk and whisk until it's thoroughly combined. Set the pan over medium-high heat and cook, whisking almost constantly, until the mixture thickens and starts to boil, about 5 minutes.

3. Continue boiling, whisking constantly, for what will feel like the longest 2 minutes of your life. Pay extra attention to the corners of the saucepan to make sure nothing scorches.

4. Strain the mixture through the sieve and stir it for a few minutes with a rubber spatula to let off some of the steam. (Stop here to use in the Raspberry Dacquoise Cake, which works best with pastry cream that's just a bit warmer than room temperature.)

5. For most other applications, or to use on its own, place a piece of plastic film or wax paper directly on the surface of the custard to prevent a skin from forming and refrigerate until firm, at least 3 hours.

STORAGE
Pastry cream will keep for up to 4 days, refrigerated with plastic film or wax paper pressed directly on its surface.

USING PASTRY CREAM

Two of the most popular ways to use pastry cream are also the easiest. Call them by their French names if you want to show off:

- Crème Légère: Mix with sweetened whipped cream to make a simple filling for cakes and pastries. I use a variation of this in the recipe for the Guava Crepe Cake.
- Crème Mousseline: Mix with softened unsalted butter as I do in the recipe for the Raspberry Dacquoise Cake.

CANDIED CITRUS PEEL

| MAKES ABOUT 1½ CUPS (270 GRAMS) | EASY |

Once you've tasted freshly candied citrus, you'll never waste your time with the store-bought drudgery.

assorted citrus, such as navel oranges, lemons, or limes	7 to 8	7 to 8
granulated sugar	2 cups	424 grams

1. Use a sharp knife to remove the peel from the fruit in wide pieces, slicing deep enough to just barely expose the flesh inside. Place the peel on the cutting board with the white side face up and carefully remove about half the pith by slicing horizontally in a sawing motion. Discard the removed pith and save the fruit for juice or snacks.

2. In a small saucepan, place the peel and add enough cold water to cover. Bring to a boil over medium heat. When it reaches a boil, drain off the water and replace with fresh cold water.

3. Return to a boil once more and cook until tender, about 10 minutes, then drain again and transfer the peel to a small bowl.

4. Bring 2 cups (500 milliliters) water and the sugar to a boil in the saucepan over medium heat, stirring just until the sugar has dissolved. Carefully add the peel to the sugar syrup and adjust the heat to a simmer.

5. Place a lid on the pot slightly ajar and cook the peels, stirring occasionally, until the pieces are translucent, about 20 minutes.

6. Remove the pan from the heat and allow the peel to cool completely in the syrup.

STORAGE

Candied peel can be stored in its syrup in a covered jar in the refrigerator for up to 1 month, or drained, air dried, and stored in an airtight container at room temperature for up to 3 months.

ANY BERRY JAM

| MAKES ABOUT 2 CUPS (640 GRAMS) | INTERMEDIATE |
| SPECIAL EQUIPMENT: CANDY THERMOMETER |

My friend Sarah taught me how to make jam, showing me the tricks to know by sight when it's cooked just right. Sarah is a jam fanatic, and she makes it the old French way. That method takes days, so I've sped it up just a bit. Because berry-based jams can be finicky, I've added lemon rind, which provides an added dose of pectin, making my method just a bit more fool-proof.

If you're going to the trouble of making jam from scratch, you might as well take the opportunity to play around with it. Ginger goes well with just about everything, but a handful of fresh herbs or some cracked black pepper can be a nice touch, too.

You can use this homemade jam in the Raspberry Almond Petit Fours (page 82), Strawberry Tamales de Dulce (page 92), Peanut Butter and Jelly Cake (page 100), and Summer Berry Shortcakes (page 122).

fresh ripe berries, such as strawberries, raspberries, blackberries, or blueberries, hulled if necessary	1 pound	454 grams
granulated sugar	1¾ to 2 cups	371 to 424 grams
coarse salt	1 pinch	1 pinch
lemon	1	1
fresh ginger, sliced, optional	1 inch	15 grams
additional fresh herbs or spices, as desired		

1. If your berries are on the larger size (I'm looking at you, supermarket strawberries), cut them into pieces that are a little more quaint. In a large saucepan, toss the berries with 1¾ cups (371 grams) of sugar and the salt. Squeeze the juice from the lemon into the pot, and then scrape the pulp off the rind with a spoon and discard. Cut the rind into 4 or 5 large pieces and add it to the pot along with the ginger, if using, or your flavoring of choice.

2. Gently heat the mixture on low, stirring with a wooden spoon just until the sugar starts to dissolve, about 2 minutes. Stop stirring before you completely break apart the more delicate fruit. Continue heating until bubbles form around the edge of the pan.

3. Simmer at this unimaginably low temperature for 5 minutes longer, then pour the mixture into a heatproof glass or ceramic bowl and let it stand at room temperature until the steam dissipates. Cover and refrigerate overnight.

4. The next day, remove the lemon rind and ginger slices or whatnot. Taste the syrup; it should be very sweet but not saccharine. If your berries

(continued)   **239**

were bland, or you plan to store the jam for a long time, add up to ¼ cup (53 grams) additional sugar.

5. Transfer the syrup to a large nonreactive pot, filling it no more than halfway (the jam will bubble up enthusiastically as it cooks).

6. Bring to a rolling boil over medium-high heat. Continue cooking the mixture, stirring constantly with a large metal spoon until it's just gelled (see below), 5 to 10 minutes, taking care not to heat the mixture above 221°F (105°C) on a candy thermometer.

7. Now would be the time to process the jam in sterilized jars, but if you're anything like me you'll just pour it into a heatproof bowl, let it cool, cover, and refrigerate.

STORAGE

Unprocessed jam will keep in the refrigerator for about 2 months.

JAM RIGHT

Jams and jellies are concoctions of fruit juice and sugar bound together by pectin, a starch found in varying quantities in all fruit. Much like cornstarch, pectin has to be heated in order to activate its thickening powers, but unlike cornstarch it deigns to work only in certain circumstances. Pectin is a self-hating polysaccharide—it literally has a negative (ionic) energy. It prefers the company of water molecules and will mesh with its own kind only under duress. We can force the kind of interaction we're looking for by adding sugar (which keeps the water otherwise engaged)* and acid (which neutralizes pectin's negative charge), giving it the push it needs to commingle.

Making jams without adding commercial pectin can be intimidating because it takes some practice to know what you're looking for. The first step is to be open to the possibility that your preserves will look somewhat different from what you might be expecting. Jams made the old-fashioned way will be a bit thinner, especially if you leave large pieces of fruit in the mix, but that's also what makes them so special.

Using a candy thermometer can help prevent overcooking, which can be detrimental to both flavor and texture, but the best tool is your jam-making spoon. If you don't have one yet, I guarantee you'll have found it by the third batch. This spoon is large, has a long handle, is not too concave, and has a smart-looking point.

Stir the mixture with your jam spoon as it cooks and test to see if it's ready to gel by scooping up some of the liquid and letting it fall off a long side of the spoon back into the pot. Start testing early and watch as the mixture changes consistency. At first it will pour like water, but as it continues cooking, the drops will change in texture. They'll start to appear gloopier, and, when ready, instead of forming individual beads of liquid, the mixture will fall off in clumps two or three drops wide. Jam from high-pectin fruits like gooseberries will fall off in sheets, but don't expect that kind of behavior from more delicate strawberries. Most important, pectin thickens as it cools, so don't overcook your jam waiting for it to set on the stove; when in doubt pull it out!

---

* Food scientists refer to this as reducing the water activity level, which also helps prevent spoilage.

PINEAPPLE JAM

| MAKES ABOUT 1 CUP (320 GRAMS) | EASY |

Don't shy away from the jalapeño. The bite and heat it provides cut through the sweetness of the pineapple and intensify the tropical flavor of this jam. Removing both the seeds and the pith will spare you from the worst of its spice, though I don't know why you would want to do that. Pineapple jam makes a wonderful accompaniment to Popovers (page 81). It deserves a place on your next cheese platter, too.

finely chopped fresh pineapple, from 1 small pineapple	3 cups	630 grams
granulated sugar	1 cup	212 grams
jalapeño, seeded and minced, to taste	1	1
coarse salt	1 pinch	1 pinch

1. In a small saucepan, place the pineapple along with 1½ cups (375 milliliters) water. Bring to a boil over medium heat, then reduce to low and simmer for 30 minutes, or until the pineapple is soft and beginning to fall apart.
2. Mash the sugar into the mixture with a potato masher. Continue cooking, mashing and stirring occasionally, until the fruit darkens and the liquid has almost completely evaporated, 35 to 40 minutes. Stir more frequently as the mixture thickens, scraping the bottom of the pot to prevent scorching.
3. Stir in the jalapeño and add the salt, then transfer the jam to a heatproof bowl to cool.

STORAGE
The jam will keep for about 1 month in the refrigerator in an airtight container.

PEPPER IN THE EYE

Getting pepper in the eye is an inevitable occurrence in our house. Eddie's remedy works best: Rub the afflicted eye with a lock of hair (anyone's will do) until the pepper oils have been wicked away and the burning stops.

CRANBERRY JAM

| MAKES ABOUT 2 CUPS (600 GRAMS) | EASY |

Bracingly tart, this jam serves as the filling for the Cranberry Yule Log (page 125) but is equally delicious on buttered dark toast.

fresh cranberries, thawed if frozen	2½ cups (about 10 ounces)	280 grams
granulated sugar	1¼ cups	265 grams
cinnamon stick	1	1
Campari, optional	2 tablespoons	30 milliliters
orange liqueur, such as Triple Sec	2 tablespoons	30 milliliters
ground cloves	1 pinch	1 pinch

1.   In a medium saucepan, combine all the ingredients with ½ cup (125 milliliters) water. Bring to a boil over medium-high heat, stirring until the sugar dissolves, about 3 minutes. The mixture will foam up dramatically and then subside.

2.   Continue boiling, stirring frequently, until the mixture is deep red and thick enough to cling to a spoon, 8 to 10 minutes.

3.   Remove the cinnamon stick. Transfer the jam to a food processor and pulse until relatively, but not completely, smooth, about 1 minute. Scrape into a heatproof bowl and cool completely before using.

STORAGE

Store the jam in a covered container in the refrigerator for up to 2 months.

APPLESAUCE

If Granny Smiths really are your favorite apple, go ahead and use them here. Granny Smiths are fine.

I don't like my apples to be fine. I want to feel like I'm biting into a glacier; I want the juice to spray out like it's been trying to escape. I want them to be sour enough to twist my tongue and sweet like maple syrup. I'd use a Stayman Winesap if it were up to me, but right now it's up to you.

Using this homemade sauce in the Applesauce Cake (page 53) makes the cake even more delicious.

your favorite apples, peeled, cored, and cut into 2-inch pieces	3 pounds	1.5 kilograms
freshly squeezed lemon juice (from ½ lemon)	1 tablespoon	15 milliliters

1. In a large sturdy pot, combine the apples, lemon juice, and ⅔ cup (166 milliliters) water. Cover with a tight-fitting lid and bring to a boil over high heat.

2. Cook, stirring occasionally, for 8 to 10 minutes. Reduce the heat to a simmer and continue cooking, covered, until the apples are completely falling apart, 5 to 10 minutes longer, adding just a touch more water if you worry things might dry up.

3. Mash the apples with a potato masher, leaving the mixture as chunky or as smooth as you like, and keep cooking, stirring constantly, until the sauce is stiff enough to hold its shape when dropped off a spoon.

4. Transfer the applesauce to a heatproof bowl to cool completely.

STORAGE

Store in an airtight container in the refrigerator for up to 1 week.

GINGER CITRUS CURD

| MAKES ABOUT ⅔ CUP (166 MILLILITERS) | EASY |

Use a Meyer lemon version of this recipe in the Kiwi and Goldenberry Saratoga Torte (page 146) and a lime one in the Passion Fruit Lime Pavlova (page 118). Store in a jar to brighten up toast for breakfast.

granulated sugar	⅓ cup	71 grams
finely grated citrus zest	1 teaspoon	2 grams
freshly squeezed citrus juice, from pink lemons, Meyer lemons, lemon lemons, limes, or what have you	⅓ cup	83 milliliters
freshly grated ginger	½ teaspoon	2.5 grams
coarse salt	¼ teaspoon	0.8 gram
large egg yolks	3	3
unsalted butter, cut into ½-inch pieces	4 tablespoons (½ stick)	57 grams

1. In a small saucepan, whisk together the sugar, zest, juice, ginger, salt, and egg yolks. Add the butter and place over medium heat, whisking constantly until the butter has melted.

2. Continue cooking and whisking over low heat until the mixture is thick enough to coat the back of a spoon, about 4 minutes. Do not allow it to boil.

3. Strain the curd through a fine-mesh sieve into a small heatproof bowl. Place a sheet of plastic film or wax paper directly on the surface to prevent a skin from forming and refrigerate until firm, about 2 hours.

STORAGE
Store in an airtight container in the refrigerator for up to 1 week.

SPECIAL SKILLS

HOW TO TRIM AND SPLIT A CAKE LAYER

A rotating cake stand makes this job a bit easier, but with composure the task can be accomplished without. I like to use a ruler to measure perfectly even layers, because I am not entirely normal.

1. Level the top of the cake by removing the dome: Using a long, serrated knife, begin by scoring a line around the entire circumference of the cake; you'll use this as a guide. Then, being careful to keep the knife as flat as possible, slice into the side of the cake in a sawing motion, rotating as you progress inward, carefully following the line you made earlier. Continue slicing until you get to the center and the dome has been freed. Save it for snacks.
2. Score a line halfway up the side of the now flat-topped cake, and then follow that line as you did earlier, sawing your way into the center, at which point the cake should be miraculously split into two pieces. I'll note that no matter how the cake looks at this point it will still taste delicious.

HOW TO ASSEMBLE A LAYER CAKE

A perfectly cylindrical layer cake requires a strong foundation of neatly trimmed layers. Once you have those, assembly is a snap:

1. For a four-layer cake that was baked in two pans, begin by placing a layer trimmed from the bottom of one cake on a rotating cake stand or serving platter, crust side down. Dollop frosting on top of the layer and spread to the edges with an offset spatula. Hold the spatula with the tip aligned to the center of the cake and spin the stand, keeping the spatula relatively still, to smooth the top of the frosting.
2. Top with the next layer of cake. Continue assembling in this manner, saving the other bottom slice of cake to use as the top layer, crust side up.
3. Use an offset spatula to smooth the frosting oozing out from the sides. Chill the cake for 15 to 20 minutes if it feels wobbly.
4. Crumb coat the cake: Spread a thin layer of frosting over the top and sides of the cake using

(continued)

an offset spatula. The cake should still be visible through the frosting, but the crumbs should be firmly trapped in place. Chill for at least 45 minutes before applying the final "beauty" coat of frosting.

HOW TO OPEN A MATURE COCONUT AND MAKE FRESH COCONUT SHAVINGS

You can purchase tools that are specially designed for opening a coconut, but unless you're planning on going into the coconut business, it may not be worthwhile. Here's how I open them:

1. Each coconut has three eyes on the top end, but only one is soft enough to pierce. Twist a clean Phillips-head screwdriver into the soft eye until you break through to the inner cavity. Shake the coconut upside down to drain the water. (The tropical juice is harvested from young coconuts, which aren't the brown, hairy ones I'm talking about here; the water in a mature coconut rarely tastes good.)

2. Place a kitchen towel in your nondominant hand and use it to hold the coconut. Using a blunt instrument like a meat mallet (full disclosure: I use a small crowbar), hit the side of the coconut in the same spot, repeatedly, until you crack the tough exterior. Then work your way around the coconut until it splits in half. Give it a quick rinse.

3. Use a sturdy butter knife to pry the flesh away from the shell, removing it in chunks. Be mindful of your fingers. If the coconut won't easily part with a piece of flesh, leave it!

4. Use a vegetable peeler to create ribbons of coconut to use as garnish. One coconut will yield about 3 cups of loosely packed shavings. (You can also grate the flesh and dry it to use in recipes instead of purchasing unsweetened shredded coconut, but come on!)

5. Store in the refrigerator in an airtight container for up to 1 week.

HOW TO MAKE CHOCOLATE CURLS

For something that looks wildly ornate, chocolate curls can be surprisingly easy to make. It's all about the temperature of the chocolate.

1. Start with a large block of chocolate; any variety will do. Gently warm it by microwaving on low power for about 10 seconds, or by briefly holding the block about 1 foot above the stove's burner set to medium. The chocolate should not appear melted.

2. Use a sharp vegetable peeler to shave the chocolate along an edge of the block. It will take some practice, but the chocolate will curl naturally when you hit a stride of shaving at the right speed and at the right temperature. You may need to rewarm the chocolate as you work.

3. Store in an airtight container in a cool, dry place for a long, long time.

HOW TO SUPREME CITRUS

Citrus supremes give you the perfect bite: a melt-in-your-mouth citrus explosion. They look nice, too.

1. Using a sharp knife, slice a thin layer off both ends of the fruit, exposing the flesh. Then stand the fruit on one end and use the knife to work your way around, removing the peel and all the white pith. You'll be left with a glowing orb of citrus.

2. Hold the fruit in your hand and use a paring knife to carefully slice on both sides of each segment, right up against the membranes that separate one from the other. Drop the naked segments into a bowl and squeeze the juice out of the skeleton of a citrus that remains in your hand over the supremes.

3. Store in a covered container in the refrigerator for a day or two.

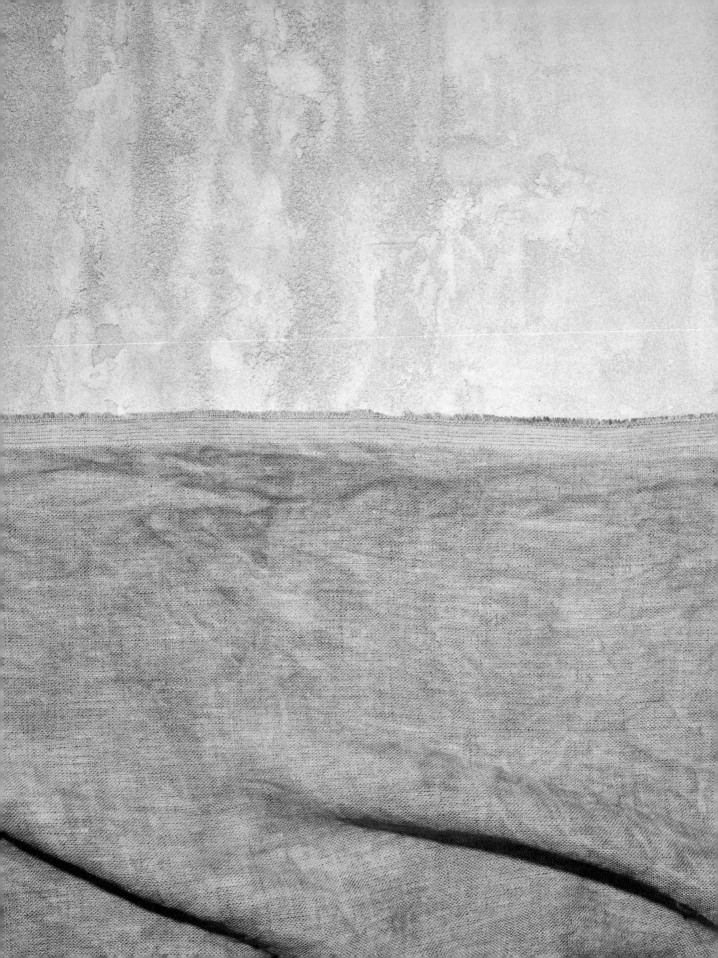

FILE UNDER: IT TAKES A VILLAGE

This was a long time coming, and I didn't go it alone. Thank you to the gaggle of recipe testers who helped make this a better book. The troupe, led by Cate Brown, with Erin Barnhart, Erick Brewer, Anika Chapin, India DeLashmutt Exsted, Barkley Galloway, Julie Novacek Godsoe, Dylan Going, Elsbeth Pancrazi, Robin Pridgen, Spencer Richards, Samantha Seneviratne, Lindsay Strand, Dana Yakoobinsky, and Janette Zapeda gracefully and graciously worked its way through these recipes, questioned my methods, and caught (hopefully all) my mistakes.

Thank you to Sharon Bowers at MBG Literary for guiding me, and to Cassie Jones, Jill Zimmerman, and the rest of the team at William Morrow for welcoming me. I'm so happy to have found you all.

Over the years, I have done photoshoots in glamorous studios, conference rooms, and a surprising number of closets. We shot this book in our apartment, and it would have been a real disaster if I hadn't had such a dedicated, nimble, and thoughtful group of friends by my side.

I couldn't be happier with these photographs by Ethan Calabrese. Thank you for toiling away on the shadows and reflections and for capturing my recipes as oddly as I could have imagined. Jess Damuck's prop styling brought my sketches to life with her hand-painted surfaces and naturally dyed linens. Not to mention the stacks, which I never saw coming. You both went above and beyond, and I am forever grateful. We would not have survived the weeks of shopping, cooking, organizing, and cleaning without the tireless work of Cate Brown, Barkley Galloway, Dylan Going, and Laurie Ellen Pellicano.

Eddie, thank you for pushing me forward, introducing me to fruit I never knew existed, and graciously welcoming a photoshoot into our home. Thank you to my parents, Jean and Tom, and to my grandparents, Bim and Sam, who watched and encouraged as I carved out this unusual path, and never questioned its worth. Adam and Laura; Emily and Michael; Danny, Liz, Anna, and Lizzie; Johnny, Marilyn, Jenny, and Adan; Pattie; Lily, Zach, Charlie, Dylan, Julian, and Adrian: Thank you for eating a combined 400-odd years of my baked goods.

To my family at Martha Stewart, thank you for taking this strange, shrieking freelancer into your kitchens and hearts, and for teaching me the ways of our weird little world. Martha, thank you for supporting this project and for your lovely contribution. Ron Ben-Israel, you taught me how to decorate cakes, but you also taught me how to run a business, which was just as important.

Thank you to the multitude of artists and chefs the world over who have influenced these recipes. The art for this book was greatly inspired by that of Mexican architect Luis Barragán (1902–1988), whose work transcends time and place, and whose sense of color, light, and texture turned the ordinary into the majestic.

A final thanks to Elena Demyanenko and Stuart Shugg, Nahvae Frost and Ed Priesner, Matt Calabrese, Mutsumi Okoshi, Alex Deng, Maxwell Tielman, Aaron Able, Kieran Dwyer, Mike Rubenstein, Lou Gruber Ceramics, Prop Workshop, and West Elm.

251

CONVERSION CHART

OVEN TEMPERATURE EQUIVALENTS

250°F = 120°C

275°F = 135°C

300°F = 150°C

325°F = 160°C

350°F = 180°C

375°F = 190°C

400°F = 200°C

425°F = 220°C

450°F = 230°C

475°F = 240°C

500°F = 260°C

MEASUREMENT EQUIVALENTS

Measurements should always be level unless directed otherwise.

⅛ teaspoon = 0.5 mL

¼ teaspoon = 1 mL

½ teaspoon = 2 mL

1 teaspoon = 5 mL

1 tablespoon = 3 teaspoons = ½ fluid ounce = 15 mL

2 tablespoons = ⅛ cup = 1 fluid ounce = 30 mL

4 tablespoons = ¼ cup = 2 fluid ounces = 62 mL

5⅓ tablespoons = ⅓ cup = 3 fluid ounces = 83 mL

8 tablespoons = ½ cup = 4 fluid ounces = 125 mL

10⅔ tablespoons = ⅔ cup = 5 fluid ounces = 166 mL

12 tablespoons = ¾ cup = 6 fluid ounces = 187 mL

16 tablespoons = 1 cup = 8 fluid ounces = 250 mL

INDEX

NOTE: Page references in *italics* indicate photographs.

A

Almond flour, about, 27
Almond paste
    Peach Bostock, 35–36, *37*
    Raspberry Almond Petit Fours, 82–84, *83*
Almonds
    Bourbon Peach Kugelhopf, 154–56, *155*
    Fig and Date Snowballs, 86, *87*
    grinding, for almond flour, 27
    Orange and Goldenberry Panforte, 74–77, *75*
    Raspberry Dacquoise Cake, 132–34, *133*
    Stollen, *176*, 177–79
Aluminum foil, 13
Ancho chile powder, about, 73
Aniseed, grinding, 202
Apples
    Applesauce, 243
    Applesauce Cake, 53–55, *54*
    Irish Soda Bread, *44*, 45–46
    Laura and Adam's Wedding Cake, *190*, 191–92
Applesauce, 243
Applesauce Cake, 53–55, *54*
Apricot(s)
    Aprigoji Mochanut Breakfast Loaves, 212–13, *213*
    Coconut Macaroon Cake, 59–61, *60*
    Poached, Sachertorte, 199–202, *201*
    Stollen, *176*, 177–79
    Stout Cake, *196*, 197–98

B

Babka, Chocolate Orange, 183–86, *187*
Baking pans, 12
Banana(s)
    Bread, *16*, 17–18
    Chocolate Caramel Roulade, 103–6, *104*
    freezing, 18
    Hummingbird Layer Cake, 115–17, *116*
    Tiramisu, *28*, 29
Beeswax wrap, 13
Bench scrapers, 12
Berry(ies). See also specific berries
    Any, Jam, *238*, 239–40
    measuring, 5
    Shortcakes, Summer, 122–24, *123*
Blackberry(ies)
    Any Berry Jam, *238*, 239–40
    Breton, 26, *27*
Blueberry(ies)
    Any Berry Jam, *238*, 239–40
    Bim's Yeast Cake, 157–58, *159*
    Ginger Studmuffins, 90–91, *91*
    Gooseberry Crumb Cakes, 41–42, *43*
Bourbon
    Laura and Adam's Wedding Cake, *190*, 191–92
    Peach Kugelhopf, 154–56, *155*
Bowl scrapers, 12
Breads
    Banana, *16*, 17–18
    Chocolate Orange Babka, 183–86, *187*
    Concord Grape Focaccia, 163–64, *165*
    Irish Soda, *44*, 45–46
    Maple Orange Cornbread, 50–52, *51*
    Panettone Tropicale, 167–71, *169*
    Peach Bostock, 35–36, *37*
Brown sugar, 5, 9
Brushes, 12
Buns, Cinnamon Raisin, 160–62, *161*
Butter, 3, 10
Buttercream
    flavoring, 233
    Swiss Meringue, *232*, 233
Buttermilk, about, 10
Buttermilk Ricotta and Peach Cake, 19–20, *21*

C

Cakes
Applesauce, 53–55, *54*

Aprigoji Mochanut Breakfast Loaves, 212–13, *213*

Blackberry Breton, 26, *27*

Blood Orange Bee-Sting, 150–53, *152*

Bourbon Peach Kugelhopf, 154–56, *155*

Breakfast, Pineapple Coconut, 66, *67*

Buttermilk Ricotta and Peach, 19–20, *21*

Chiffon, Perfect, 228–29, *229*

Chocolate, Cherry, and Orange, 203–5, *204*

Chocolate Caramel Banana Roulade, 103–6, *104*

Coconut Apricot Macaroon, 59–61, *60*

Coconut Cielo, *128,* 129–31

Cranberry Yule Log, 125–26, *127*

Crumb, Blueberry Gooseberry, 41–42, *43*

Crumb, Poached Pear and Quince, *38,* 39–40

Fig, Port, and Chocolate, 209–11, *210*

Guava Crepe, 141–42, *143*

Honey Yuzu Kasutera, 22–24, *23*

Horchata Sorbet and Roasted Plum, 135–36, *137*

Hummingbird Layer, 115–17, *116*

Jamaican Black, 206–8, *207*

Key Lime, 112–14, *113*

layer, assembling, 247–48

layer, trimming and splitting, 247

Mamey Cheesecake, 107–8, *109*

Mango Coconut Cashew Bites, 78, *79*

Nectarine Kuchen, 180–82, *181*

Peanut Butter and Jelly, 100–102, *101*

Poached Apricot Sachertorte, 199–202, *201*

Pomegranate Molasses and Cherry, 214–17, *215*

Pound, Coconut, 62, *63*

Pound, Polenta, with Spiced Mandarins, 56–58, *57*

Raspberry Dacquoise, 132–34, *133*

Rosca de Reyes, 172–75, *173*

Semolina, with Fennel and Raisins, *32,* 33–34

Snacking, Hazelnut Plum, 30–31, *31*

Sticky Toffee Date, 193–94, *195*

Stollen, *176,* 177–79

Stout, *196,* 197–98

Tea, Raspberry, 47–49, *48*

Ume-Shiso Watermelon Frozen Yogurt, *138,* 139–40

Wedding, Laura and Adam's, *190,* 191–92

Yeast, Bim's, 157–58, *159*

Cake testers, 12

Candied Citrus Peel

buying, 175

Flaming Figgy Pudding, 218–21, *219*

fresh, cooking with, 175

Jamaican Black Cake, 206–8, *207*

Panettone Tropicale, 167–71, *169*

recipe for, 236, *237*

Rosca de Reyes, 172–75, *173*

Stollen, *176,* 177–79

Caramel Chocolate Banana Roulade, 103–6, *104*

Cardamom seeds, grinding, 11

Cashew Mango Coconut Bites, 78, *79*

Cheese. *See* Cream cheese; Mascarpone cheese

Cheesecake, Mamey, 107–8, *109*

Cherry(ies)

Chocolate, and Orange Cake, 203–5, *204*

dried, buying, 12

Jamaican Black Cake, 206–8, *207*

and Pomegranate Molasses Cake, 214–17, *215*

Stout Cake, *196,* 197–98

Chiffon Cake, Perfect, 228–29, *229*

Chocolate

Banana Tiramisu, *28,* 29

buying, 11

Caramel Banana Roulade, 103–6, *104*

Cherry, and Orange Cake, 203–5, *204*

couverture, about, 11

Cranberry Yule Log, 125–26, *127*

curls, creating, 248

Fig, and Port Cake, 209–11, *210*

measuring, 5

Orange and Goldenberry Panforte, 74–77, *75*

Orange Babka, 183–86, *187*

Poached Apricot Sachertorte, 199–202, *201*

Raspberry Almond Petit Fours, 82–84, *83*
Raspberry Dacquoise Cake, 132–34, *133*
Stout Cake, *196*, 197–98
tempering versus melting, 84
working with, 84
Cinnamon Raisin Buns, 160–62, *161*
Citrus. *See also* Candied Citrus Peel
    Curd, Ginger, 244, *245*
    how to supreme, 248–49
    zesting, 12
Coconut
    Apricot Macaroon Cake, 59–61, *60*
    Cielo Cake, *128*, 129–31
    Fig and Date Snowballs, 86, *87*
    Hummingbird Layer Cake, 115–17, *116*
    Mango Cashew Bites, 78, *79*
    Pineapple Breakfast Cakes, 66, *67*
    Pound Cake, 62, *63*
    shavings, creating, 248
    whole, cracking open, 248
Compost, 13
Concord Grape Focaccia, 163–64, *165*
Confectioners' sugar, 4, 9
Cornmeal
    Italian-style, 6
    Maple Orange Cornbread, 50–52, *51*
    measuring, 5
    stone-ground, 9
Cornstarch, measuring, 4
Corn syrup, science of, 136
Couverture chocolate, about, 11
Cranberry
    Jam, 242
    Pecan Muffins, Jumbo, *68*, 69–70
    Yule Log, 125–26, *127*
Cream, heavy, 10
Cream Cheese
    buying, 10
    Chocolate Caramel Banana Roulade, 103–6, *104*
    Frosting, Tangy, 230, *231*
    Hummingbird Layer Cake, 115–17, *116*
    Key Lime Cake, 112–14, *113*
    Mamey Cheesecake, 107–8, *109*
    Pumpkin Cupcakes, 71–73, *72*
Crème fraîche, buying, 10
Crème Légère, 235

Crème Mousseline, 235
Crepe Cake, Guava, 141–42, *143*
Cupcakes, Pumpkin, 71–73, *72*
Curd, Ginger Citrus, 244, *245*
Currant(s)
    Flaming Figgy Pudding, 218–21, *219*
    Irish Soda Bread, *44*, 45–46
    Jamaican Black Cake, 206–8, *207*
    Orange Zaleti, 96–97, *97*
    Stollen, *176*, 177–79

D

Dacquoise Cake, Raspberry, 132–34, *133*
Dairy, for recipes, 10
Date
    and Fig Snowballs, 86, *87*
    Sticky Toffee Cakes, 193–94, *195*
Digital scales, 5

E

Eggs, 3, 12
Extracts, 5, 12

F

Fats, types of, 10
Fennel and Raisins, Semolina Cake with, *32*, 33–34
Fig(s)
    and Date Snowballs, 86, *87*
    Flaming Figgy Pudding, 218–21, *219*
    Port, and Chocolate Cake, 209–11, *210*
Finger limes, about, 121
Flambéeing cakes, 221
Flours, 4, 6–9
Focaccia, Concord Grape, 163–64, *165*
Food waste, 13
Fools, Strawberry, *110*, 111
Frosting
    Cream Cheese, Tangy, 230, *231*
    Swiss Meringue Buttercream, *232*, 233
Fruit. See also Fruitcakes; specific fruits
Fruitcakes
    Aprigoji Mochanut Breakfast Loaves, 212–13, *213*
    Fig, Port, and Chocolate Cake, 209–11, *210*

Fruitcakes (*continued*)
    Jamaican Black Cake, 206–8, *207*
    Laura and Adam's Wedding Cake, *190*,
       191–92
    Pomegranate Molasses and Cherry Cake,
       214–17, *215*

G

Ganache, note about, 106
Ginger
    Blueberry Studmuffins, 90–91, *91*
    Citrus Curd, 244, *245*
    Mango Coconut Cashew Bites, 78, *79*
    Poached Apricot Sachertorte, 199–202,
       201
    Pomegranate Molasses and Cherry Cake,
       214–17, *215*
    Stout Cake, *196*, 197–98
Goji berries
    Aprigoji Mochanut Breakfast Loaves,
       212–13, *213*
Goldenberry
    and Kiwi Saratoga Torte, 146, *147*
    and Orange Panforte, 74–77, *75*
Gooseberry Blueberry Crumb Cakes, 41–42, *43*
Grape, Concord, Focaccia, 163–64, *165*
Guava Crepe Cake, 141–42, *143*

H

Hazelnut(s)
    Aprigoji Mochanut Breakfast Loaves,
       212–13, *213*
    Orange and Goldenberry Panforte, 74–77,
       75
    Plum Snacking Cake, 30–31, *31*
Herbs, measuring, 5
Honey Yuzu Kasutera Cake, 22–24, *23*
Horchata and Roasted Plum Sorbet Cake, 135–36,
    137
Hummingbird Layer Cake, 115–17, *116*

I

Ingredients, 6–12
    dairy, 10
    fats, 10
    flours, 6–9
    measuring, 4–5
    room temperature, 3
    salt, 10
    sweeteners, 9
    yeast, 10–11
Irish Soda Bread, *44*, 45–46

J

Jamaican Black Cake, 206–8, *207*
Jams
    Any Berry, *238*, 239–40
    Cranberry, 242
    Peanut Butter and Jelly Cake, 100–102, *101*
    Pineapple, *238*, 241
    preparing, tips for, 240

K

Kasutera Cake, Honey Yuzu, 22–24, *23*
Key Lime Cake, 112–14, *113*
Kitchen tools, 12–13
Kiwi and Goldenberry Saratoga Torte, 146, *147*
Kugelhopf, Bourbon Peach, 154–56, *155*

L

Ladyfingers
    Banana Tiramisu, *28*, 29
    Kiwi and Goldenberry Saratoga Torte, 146,
       147
    recipe for, *226*, 227
    Strawberry Fools, *110*, 111
Leaveners, measuring, 5
Lemon(s)
    Candied Citrus Peel, 236, *237*
    Ginger Citrus Curd, 244, *245*
    peel, tossing with sugar, 49
Lime(s)
    Candied Citrus Peel, 236, *237*
    finger, about, 121
    Ginger Citrus Curd, 244, *245*
    Key, Cake, 112–14, *113*
    Passion Fruit Pavlova, 118–21, *119*
Liquids, measuring, 4

M

Macaroon Cake, Coconut Apricot, 59–61, *60*
Mace, about, 77
Mandarins, Spiced, Polenta Pound Cake with,
    56–58, *57*

Mango(es)
    Coconut Cashew Bites, 78, *79*
    Panettone Tropicale, 167–71, *169*
Maple Orange Cornbread, 50–52, *51*
Marzipan
    Stollen, *176*, 177–79
Masa harina
    about, 6
    Strawberry Tamales de Dulce, 92–95, *93*
Mascarpone cheese
    Banana Tiramisu, *28*, 29
    Blood Orange Bee-Sting Cake, 150–53, *152*
    buying, 10
Measuring cups, 4
Measuring spoons, 5
Meringue
    Kiwi and Goldenberry Saratoga Torte, 146,
        147
    Passion Fruit Lime Pavlova, 118–21, *119*
    Raspberry Dacquoise Cake, 132–34, *133*
Milk, 3, 10
Mixers, 12
Muffins
    Blueberry Ginger Studmuffins, 90–91, *91*
    Jumbo Cranberry Pecan, *68*, 69–70
    Orange Zucchini, 88–89, *89*

N

Nectarine Kuchen, 180–82, *181*
Nutmeg, 12, 77
Nuts. See also specific nuts
    measuring, 5
    toasting, 18

O

Oats
    Blueberry Gooseberry Crumb Cakes,
        41–42, *43*
    Jumbo Cranberry Pecan Muffins, *68*,
        69–70
Offset spatulas, 12
Orange liqueur
    Blood Orange Bee-Sting Cake, 150–53, *152*
    Chocolate, Cherry, and Orange Cake,
        203–5, *204*
    Chocolate Orange Babka, 183–86, *187*
    Cranberry Jam, *238*, 242

Cranberry Yule Log, 125–26, *127*
Orange Zucchini Muffins, 88–89, *89*
Polenta Pound Cake with Spiced
    Mandarins, 56–58, *57*
Pomegranate Molasses and Cherry Cake,
    214–17, *215*
Strawberry Fools, *110*, 111
Orange(s)
    Blood, Bee-Sting Cake, 150–53, *152*
    Candied Citrus Peel, 236, *237*
    Chocolate, and Cherry Cake, 203–5, *204*
    Chocolate Babka, 183–86, *187*
    Currant Zaleti, 96–97, *97*
    Flaming Figgy Pudding, 218–21, *219*
    and Goldenberry Panforte, 74–77, *75*
    Jamaican Black Cake, 206–8, *207*
    Maple Cornbread, 50–52, *51*
    Panettone Tropicale, 167–71, *169*
    Polenta Pound Cake with Spiced
        Mandarins, 56–58, *57*
    Rosca de Reyes, 172–75, *173*
    Semolina Cake with Fennel and Raisins, *32*,
        33–34
    Zucchini Muffins, 88–89, *89*
Oven temperature, 3

P

Panettone Tropicale, 167–71, *169*
Panforte, Orange and Goldenberry, 74–77, *75*
Pan Goo, 224, *225*
Parchment paper, 13
Passion Fruit Lime Pavlova, 118–21, *119*
Pastry Cream
    popular ways to use, 235
    recipe for, 234–35, *235*
Pavlova, Passion Fruit Lime, 118–21, *119*
Peach(es)
    Bostock, 35–36, *37*
    Bourbon Kugelhopf, 154–56, *155*
    and Buttermilk Ricotta Cake, 19–20,
        21
Peanut Butter and Jelly Cake, 100–102, *101*
Pear(s)
    Laura and Adam's Wedding Cake, *190*,
        191–92
    Poached, and Quince Crumb Cake, *38*,
        39–40

Pecan(s)
    Bim's Yeast Cake, 157–58, *159*
    Cranberry Muffins, Jumbo, *68,* 69–70
    Fig, Port, and Chocolate Cake, 209–11, *210*
    Flaming Figgy Pudding, 218–21, *219*
    Hummingbird Layer Cake, 115–17, *116*
    Laura and Adam's Wedding Cake, *190,*
        191–92
    Stout Cake, *196,* 197–98
Pepper oils in the eye, remedy for, 241
Pineapple
    Coconut Breakfast Cakes, 66, *67*
    Hummingbird Layer Cake, 115–17, *116*
    Jam, *238,* 241
    Jam, Popovers with, *80,* 81
Plastics, avoiding, 13
Plastic wrap, 13
Plum
    Hazelnut Snacking Cake, 30–31, *31*
    Roasted, and Horchata Sorbet Cake,
        135–36, *137*
Polenta
    Orange Currant Zaleti, 96–97, *97*
    Pound Cake with Spiced Mandarins, 56–58,
        57
    quick cooking, about, 6
Pomegranate Molasses and Cherry Cake, 214–17,
    215
Popovers with Pineapple Jam, *80,* 81
Port
    Fig, and Chocolate Cake, 209–11, *210*
    Fig and Date Snowballs, 86, *87*
Pound Cake
    Coconut, 62, *63*
    Polenta, with Spiced Mandarins, 56–58,
        57
Prunes
    Jamaican Black Cake, 206–8, *207*
Pudding, Flaming Figgy, 218–21, *219*
Pumpkin
    Cupcakes, 71–73, *72*
    puree, measuring, 5

Q

Quince and Poached Pear Crumb Cake, *38,*
    39–40

R

Raisin(s)
    Cinnamon Buns, 160–62, *161*
    and Fennel, Semolina Cake with, *32,* 33–34
    Jamaican Black Cake, 206–8, *207*
    Stollen, *176,* 177–79
Raspberry(ies)
    Almond Petit Fours, 82–84, *83*
    Any Berry Jam, *238,* 239–40
    Dacquoise Cake, 132–34, *133*
    Tea Cake, 47–49, *48*
Rasp graters, 12
Ricotta, Buttermilk, and Peach Cake, 19–20, *21*
Rolling pins, 12
Rosca de Reyes, 172–75, *173*
Rubber spatulas, 12
Rulers, 12
Rum
    Aprigoji Mochanut Breakfast Loaves,
        212–13, *213*
    Banana Tiramisu, *28,* 29
    Chocolate Caramel Banana Roulade,
        103–6, *104*
    Flaming Figgy Pudding, 218–21, *219*
    Jamaican Black Cake, 206–8, *207*
    Pomegranate Molasses and Cherry Cake,
        214–17, *215*
    Sticky Toffee Date Cakes, 193–94, *195*
    Stollen, *176,* 177–79

S

Sachertorte, Poached Apricot, 199–202, *201*
Salt, 5, 10, 106
Semolina Cake with Fennel and Raisins, *32,*
    33–34
Semolina flour, about, 6–9
Shortcakes, Summer Berry, 122–24, *123*
Sieves, 13
Silicone baking mats, 13
Snowballs, Fig and Date, 86, *87*
Sour cream, 5, 10
Spatulas, 12
Spelt flour, about, 9
Sticky Toffee Date Cakes, 193–94, *195*
Stollen, *176,* 177–79
Stout Cake, *196,* 197–98

Strawberry(ies)
    Any Berry Jam, *238*, 239–40
    Fools, *110*, 111
    Peanut Butter and Jelly Cake, 100–102, *101*
    Tamales de Dulce, 92–95, *93*
Sugared lemon peel, 49
Sugars, 5, 9
Sweeteners, types of, 9
Swiss Meringue Buttercream, *232*, 233
Syrups, 9

T

Tamales de Dulce, Strawberry, 92–95, *93*
Thermometers, 13
Tiramisu, Banana, *28*, 29
Tools, 12–13

U

Ume-Shiso Watermelon Frozen Yogurt Cake, *138*, 139–40

V

Vanilla extract, 12

W

Walnuts
    Applesauce Cake, 53–55, *54*
    Banana Bread, *16*, 17–18
    Cinnamon Raisin Buns, 160–62, *161*
    Jamaican Black Cake, 206–8, *207*

Watermelon Ume-Shiso Frozen Yogurt Cake, *138*, 139–40
Weight, measuring by, 5
Whiskey
    Irish Soda Bread, *44*, 45–46
Whisks, 13
White chocolate
    Guava Crepe Cake, 141–42, *143*
    Passion Fruit Lime Pavlova, 118–21, *119*
Wire cooling racks, 13

Y

Yeast, 10–11, 159
Yogurt
    buying, 10
    Mamey Cheesecake, 107–8, *109*
    measuring, 5
    Semolina Cake with Fennel and Raisins, *32*, 33–34
    Ume-Shiso Watermelon Frozen, Cake, *138*, 139–40
Yuzu
    Honey Kasutera Cake, 22–24, *23*
    juice, about, 24

Z

Zaleti, Orange Currant, 96–97, *97*
Zesting, 12
Zucchini Orange Muffins, 88–89, *89*

HarperCollins books may be purchased for educational, business, or sales promotional use. For information, please email the Special Markets Department at SPsales@ harpercollins.com.

FIRST EDITION

DESIGNED BY RENATA DE OLIVEIRA
PHOTOGRAPHY BY ETHAN CALABRESE

Library of Congress Cataloging-in-Publication Data has been applied for.

ISBN 978-0-06-297745-8

20 21 22 23 24   WOR   10 9 8 7 6 5 4 3 2 1